The Authorities

Powerful Wisdom from Leaders in the Field

ALANA LEONE

Pushy Coaching & Training
Award Winning Author

AuthoritiesPress

Publisher
Authorities Press
Markham, ON
Canada

Printed in the United States and Canada.

FOREWORD

Experts are to be admired for their knowledge, but they often remain unrecognized by the general public because they save their information and insights for paying customers and clients. There are many experts in a given field, but their impact is limited to the handful of people with whom they work.

Unlike experts, authorities share their knowledge and expertise far more broadly, so they make a big impact on the world. Authorities become known and admired as leading experts and, as such, typically do very well economically and professionally. Most authorities are also mature enough to know that part of the joy of monetary success is the accompanying moral and spiritual obligation to give back.

Many people want to learn and work with well-respected and generous authorities, but don't always know where to find them. They may be known to their peers, or within a specific community, but have not had the opportunity to reach a wider audience. At one time, they might have submitted a proposal to the For Dummies or Chicken Soup for the Soul series of books, but it's now almost impossible to get accepted as a new author in such branded book series.

It is more than fitting that Raymond Aaron, an internationally known and respected authority in his own right, would be the one to recognize the need for a new venue in which authorities could share their considerable knowledge with readers everywhere. As the only author ever to be included in both of the book series mentioned above, Raymond has had the opportunity to give back and he understands how crucial it is for authorities to have a platform from which to share their expertise.

I have known and worked with Raymond for a number of years and consider him a valued friend and talented coach. He knows how to spot talented and knowledgeable people and he desires to see them prosper. Over the years, success coaching and speaking engagements around the world have made it possible for Raymond to meet many of these talented authorities. He recognizes and relates to their passion and enthusiasm for what they do, as well as their desire to share what they know. He tells me that's why he created this new nonfiction branded book series, The Authorities.

Dr. Nido Qubein
President, High Point University

TABLE OF CONTENTS

INTRODUCTION

This book introduces you to *The Authorities* — individuals who have distinguished themselves in life and in business. Authorities make a big impact on the world. Authorities are leaders in their chosen fields. Authorities typically do very well financially, and are evolved enough to know that part of the joy of monetary success is the accompanying social, moral and spiritual obligation to give back.

Authorities are not just outstanding. They are also *known* to be outstanding.

This additional element begins to explain the difference between two strategic business and life concepts — one that seems great, but isn't, and the other that fills in the essential missing gap of the first.

The first concept is "the expert."

What is an expert? The real definition is …

EXPERT: *a person who knows stuff*

People who have attained a very senior academic degree (like a PhD or an MD) definitely know stuff. People who read voraciously and retain what they read definitely know stuff. Unfortunately, just because you know stuff does not mean that anyone respects the fact that you do. Even though some experts are successful, alas, most are not — because knowing stuff is not enough.

Well, then, what is the missing piece?

What the expert lacks, "the authority" has. The authority both knows stuff and is *known* to know stuff. So, more simply …

AUTHORITY: *a person who is known as an expert*

The difference is not subtle. The difference is not merely semantic. The difference is enormous.

When it comes to this subject, there are actually three categories in which people fall:

- People who don't know much and are unsuccessful in life and in business. Most people fall in this category.

- People who know stuff, but still don't leave much of a footprint in the world. There are a lot of people like this.

- Experts who are also *known* as experts become authorities and authorities are always wondrously successful. Authorities are able to contribute more to humanity through both their chosen work and their giving back.

This book is about the highest category, *The Authorities* — people who have reached the peak in their field and are known as such.

You will definitely know some of *The Authorities* in this book, especially since there are some world-famous ones. Others are just as exceptional, but you may not yet know about them. Our featured author, Alana Leone, is one of these authors.

After starting a family, Alana built a million-dollar directional drilling business, which is now a legacy to her children. She has reinvented herself and now trains others to take action to get what they desire. She started a coaching and training business that is nationally known where she works with people all over the world. She leads classes for certification where she teaches people to be self-performing. Her classes focus on shifting some of the ways the mind thinks and creating processes for taking action. Then her program teaches how to build a team and create change in our world by training you to be a helper for those who are searching. One of Alana Leone's beliefs is that we keep what we have—happiness, tools, strategies, wisdom, love—by passing it on.

Your life is full of moments where you have to decide where to go next. *Five Key Elements for Success* is a proven strategy to achieve all you desire over and over, with ease and happiness. Your journey through life is unique, and the baggage of the past can negatively impact the choices you make in your future. Read the *Five Key Elements for Success* chapter by Alana Leone, as she will help you identify areas where your past experiences could be influencing your present and how to change it.

Right from the start, Alana focuses on the power you have over your thoughts. Then, she gives you the motivation to act! Each element provides several critical takeaways. These points are tools that will help you address your past hurts, and the negative feelings you carry throughout your life. These points will guide you to be ready for you to take action that will create positive results. Alana shares tools meant to help you understand why you react in various ways and how to create change.

As you read through this chapter, meditate on areas of your life and be honest about whether the examples fit. Alana's voice can help you cut through the clutter and negativity to find your power and put it to use.

No matter where you are in your life, you have the power to choose a new path or new way of thinking. It requires shifting your patterns and retraining your mind, and the results are worth the effort. Take a journey of self-discovery, one that can lead you to a different way of thinking and a brighter future!

They are *The Authorities*. Learn from them. Connect with them. Let them uplift you. Learning from them and working with them is the secret ingredient for success which may well allow you to rise to the level of Authority soon.

To be considered for inclusion in a subsequent edition of *The Authorities*, register to attend a future event at www.aaron.com/events where you will be interviewed and considered.

Five Key Elements for Success

Shift to the Next Level

ALANA LEONE

There are moments in our lives when we have an opportunity to change our path, to explore in a new direction, and to step out into the unknown. Too often, doubts and fears can take hold in our lives, limiting the risks we take and the amount of success we can claim.

I want you to change all that. I don't offer this lightly. With the power of opening your mind to peak performance thinking, you are putting yourself on the path to generate the success you want in your life.

Now, to be clear, all of us have different definitions of success. You are already successful now in some areas of your life. Now let's take that to the next level.

It involves laser focusing on what you want instead of being stuck with what you don't want. By creating a drive to pursue your desires and ditching your limiting decisions and beliefs, your life will take on a whole new meaning. You leave the plateau and reach new heights. You feel energized! It takes stepping outside of your comfort zone and overcoming challenges instead of creating obstacles. It takes climbing one step at a time to the next peak.

As part of my work, I assist people to make the transition away from their fixed thinking and their inability to take advantage of the possibilities around them. Instead, I invite them to open their minds and explore what success they can claim through a shift to next level thinking. I give them the strategies, tools, and behaviors to be able to do it themselves.

Part of a mindset shift involves removing the sting of failure. I often tell my grandson, "What a lie of the mind it is to think you are going to start something brand new and you are not going to fail."

It is what you do with the failure that gets you to the next peak or leaves you stuck on the plateau. Take what you learn, implement it, and then do it again. When you take failure as feedback, it becomes less personal. If it is something you have decided you want, you will do it. Look at when you first learned to drive. Did you fail? If you are like me, then you likely did fail every day until the day you didn't. I didn't quit. You likely didn't either. I took what I learned and got back behind the wheel. This process is a strategy for success. It's a tool you already used in other areas of your life — only, you forgot.

Your mind likes to put you down and keep you safe. Mine too! Now I say thank you to my mind and make a shift to the next level. I have control over my mind, not the other way around. Too often, we attach negative emotions to failure. Instead, recognize it as a positive learning experience, one that is meant to assist your growth. There is potential in all of us to change, to alter ourselves and our circumstances. Too often, we allow our circumstances to turn into a much bigger obstacle, one that quickly becomes a blockade in achieving our goals and desires.

How can you push through the blockade? First, determine whether you are thinking with a fixed mindset or an open, curious one. As you explore your thinking patterns, you will be able to blast through the obstacles and blockades your mind has created.

As part of this journey, I am going to share with you the importance of five key elements for success. You can achieve success with these elements just by taking one step, then another — to shift to the next level.

PUSH THROUGH TO SUCCESS

When you operate with a fixed mindset, there are a few elements that come into play. One of the first is how you talk to yourself. In a fixed mindset, your self-talk tends to have a negative aspect to it. Time and again, you tell yourself that was a stupid decision. , You ask yourself "Why did you think you could do that?" or "Don't take the risk!" There is a lot of "No, no" and "Wait, wait" throughout that list.

Plus, when your self-talk is full of negativity, and on a constant repeat, then you quickly begin to believe what you are telling yourself. A vicious cycle starts, one that cannot stop unless you make a conscious effort to do so.

That self-talk also impacts your reality. After all, if you think you are not capable, then your subconscious mind is going to seek out the evidence of that from your surroundings. It reinforces that negativity.

Your subconscious mind is listening to the words you say. It believes that these words are what you want. That is why I cannot say it enough: Think and say what you want, not what you don't want. I catch myself doing this all the time. I frequently ask myself, "Is that what I want? If not, then change it right now!" Once you spend time focused on the positive or what you want, then you will see it leak out of your mind through your mouth. Then it moves from your mouth to your actions. It is a beautiful sight and sound. Once you experience it over and over, you feel amazing.

When you push through a negative mindset, you make the conscious choice to focus your thoughts around a positive viewpoint. There are many tools for your toolbox in the world today, and you have to be willing to use them. You gain the discipline to keep on top of it. Look at football or any sport you love. The coach is there every game and every practice to push through negative mindsets and motivate the team. The coach doesn't come at the first part of the year to give the team a pep talk and then nothing the rest of the year! He constantly pushes and reminds the team, "You got this!"

How can you make these new decisions? The first part of any new strategy is recognizing what decisions to eliminate. Recognize that eliminating one negative decision or belief means another positive decision of belief must replace it. Otherwise, within the vacuum, your old ways are likely to return.

Next level thinking is about pushing yourself to identify those unproductive patterns within your subconscious way of thinking and shifting them into what you desire. Often the best way to address limiting decisions and beliefs is through a conscious dig into your past.

Past experiences and decisions create limiting decisions and beliefs. In turn, that past creates a root cause, likely within the years of your life up to age seven. In fact, without learning from the past issues, you are susceptible to another limiting decision or belief based on the same root cause. Think of a tree with lots of fruit on it. You automatically assume that the roots of the tree are flourishing. However, there may be rot that is not visible to the naked eye. The same is true of your life. There may be root causes that keep you from flourishing but are not easily spotted.

Let's start with examining what root causes are and how to tear out those rotting roots and replace them with nourished, healthy roots for your life and your business.

ELEMENT #1 - ROOT CAUSES

First, let's start with how you are thinking now and the impact it has on your life.

We all have a story that starts with detailed events and ends pointing the finger at someone else, declaring them guilty of some misdeed. In many ways, this is the story of self. What you believe about yourself and others in your story gets ingrained further through a spiral of negative thoughts and actions.

The more we talk about this, the deeper it gets driven. At some point, the body starts to feel the emotions in other ways, such as sickness, depression, rage, and anxiety. A trip to the doctor for a pharmaceutical cure focuses on the ailing body, but not the root cause in the spirit.

As you think back to the main events of your story, I would like you to come up with an age when an event occurred. Are you two, four, six, ten or twelve? Now I would like you to think about how long you have been preparing and restructuring this story of the past into your conceptualized self. This part creates an identity. There is usually a lot of emotional baggage, often sadness, anger, fear, hurt, and guilt. You end up feeling trapped and making decisions based on those emotions. Thus, you create a pattern of self-sabotage or procrastination. You want the procrastination to go away, but it goes much deeper than just procrastination. The cause is deep in the soil and the roots, corroding and rotting them further.

It becomes a deadweight in your life, one that keeps you from pushing forward. How long do you want to be trapped by those emotions, the hurts, and the negative energy that comes from these stories in your life? How long is enough for you to hurt before you are done with it? When do you decide that it is time for you to have the freedom to push forward?

Our childhoods are not dictated by us, but by the people who surround us. Parents, extended family, and others impact who we are and the experiences that we have. Those experiences shape our beliefs about ourselves and who we are in the world. However, there are also those of us who grow up in situations based on past hurts. Those older adults do not know how to address their past hurts, so they pass those hurts onto their children. It becomes a generational hurt, one that has roots so deep it can be hard even to address them.

They have all done the best they can with their experiences. This reality may be hard to hear, and it doesn't give people a pass for being this way. However, they were that way, and now it is up to you to push forward and make different choices because you can see a different path. The best thing you could do to get back at them is to have massive success and joy.

Let the events in your past propel you to impact your present and future for good. You might want to break that cycle of negativity and rot. However, that can be difficult because you don't know any other way to think, feel, or behave. What do you do?

Our society is changing, and the next generations are determined not to carry that heavy emotional and mental baggage into the future. Their choice to address these issues or root causes means developing new tools. My passion is to share these tools with others for the next generations and our nations, thus transforming our world with information and education.

One aspect of shifting our thinking is in recognizing new teachings about how to harness the power of your mind. Some people were taught about the mind, how powerful it is, and how it helps to keep us safe. Some people were taught that we have control over the actions of our mind. We are not powerless over our thoughts. You are programmed with certain beliefs and values. The good news is, if you want to change the old programming, then you can.

Shifting your negative beliefs and useless values can take courage. In the end, however, it is a very cleansing experience. By that I mean, when you settle past hurts, you can address your emotional baggage and set it down for good. How can you set that past baggage down?

Part of that is based around the principle of forgiveness. When you forgive someone, you free yourself from any power they might have over you, mentally and emotionally. Forgiveness involves letting go of any resentment and refusing to allow them to hold you emotionally hostage. Often, while you might be hurting, they might not even still be thinking of you or even remember the hurt that they caused. That person might even justify it in their minds, believing that it was for your good.

In the end, you have the power to decide how long you are willing to let the actions of others impact you. It is up to you now to take responsibility in your choice to stay stuck or push forward. It is not always easy to make that decision and stick with it. Emotions can come into play, essentially sabotaging your efforts. When you choose a path and stick with it, then you find that shift in your thinking. The most effective way is to remove the emotion around the event and come up with some learnings. This process is what I have mastered. Do not let your mind come up with excuses. Rid yourself of the past burdens and fly free.

My passion is to give people tools to clear those emotions. It is important to remove the toxic negative emotion — the root cause — by filling your roots with a powerful positive emotion. You need to give yourself the tools to drain the emotion of a memory. Doing so will allow you to be at peace with those events and then push forward with your life.

Another important point is that you can have positive root causes as well. Those are the memories and emotional ties that helped you understand your purpose or gave you a belief system that continues to support you.

Positive roots can also be a way to connect with others. When you have a positive experience, it tends to color your day and make you more inclined to try and do the same for others. Shifting your thinking involves taking those positive root experiences and allowing them to help you gain a deeper understanding of yourself and to deal with others in a kind, generous, and loving way.

I love the metaphor of the tree. Roots are so critical to the life of the tree. Without proper care, then the tree will eventually die from a lack of food, water, and stability. Think of all the ways that your roots provide stability in your life. They ground you, give you a sense of the world you live in, and social rules that help you to operate in that world. Negative root causes can be damaging to your internal root system, thus threatening your stability and the means by which you can continue to grow and flourish in your life. Granted, it is possible to save the tree, but that means you need to do the hard work to address the rot. Addressing rot involves self-care and hard work, as well as creating new patterns that will nourish healthy roots.

Essentially, addressing rot can save the tree. Plus, when you take the time to care for your roots, both positive and negative, then you will find that your tree is healthier and more stable.

When you see a tree with toxic roots — the leaves are brown and sparse — there is evidence of compromised stability. It is dying a slow painful death. After some time, the tree will fall over in a windstorm. Move to a picture of a tall, healthy tree with strong roots. This tree will have a lot of leaves and be strong and confident in its stature. It will also have big, juicy, and excellent tasting fruit, and live a long, healthy life.

The healthier the roots, the more productive the tree and the more excellent the fruit. Your life can be the one you have always imagined, but only if you are willing to change how you interact with the world by addressing the various root causes within your background. I want you to be a healthy tree, not one with sparse and brown leaves, struggling to survive the windstorms of life.

Now you need to look at your roots. Are they healthy or can you detect some signs of rot? When you detect that rot, it is important to address it right away. Next level thinking means not allowing thoughts, emotions, and events to fester and cause further damage. At the same time, when you address those root causes, then you are dealing with the damage already done.

I want you to understand that it is possible to get your roots healthy and keep you growing and thriving. Next level thinking focuses on helping you understand yourself better, including why you react a certain way, and why certain situations trigger specific emotions. There are always root causes.

Addressing them will help clear the way to change how you react not only in these situations but in other stressful circumstances and wind storms.

I am passionate about helping individuals detect the rot in their roots and then ferret it out. Once you clear the damaged roots, the tree (you) can flourish and grow toward your goals and dreams without that dead weight. Part of that process is not only clearing the negative, but also helping new roots grow in place of those old roots.

Too often, people focus on those old root causes and make them the obstacle that keeps them from pushing forward and embracing new ways of thinking. However, when you decide that you will address those root causes and that they will no longer be obstacles, then you can begin to see the new possibilities that await you! You begin to look for new roots.

Recap:
- Root causes impact our beliefs and values, how we think, and our self-talk.
- Addressing root causes can leave room for new growth.
- Work with me to clear out your rot and clear the obstacles in your path.

ELEMENT #2 - NEW ROOTS

To be even more successful, you need to recognize the responsibility you have in your life to choose change. You are in charge and have the power to shift your beliefs and values. Your experiences give you valuable learnings, so you can reach out to expand and flourish. Your mindset controls your behavior. When you take the knowledge and leave behind the emotional sabotage, you will train your brain to search and keep busy looking for positive information.

It is like a puppy that is full of energy. When you aren't giving the puppy something productive to do, then it will eat your shoes. Keep your mind busy with actionable thoughts and productivity, thus training it to work for you and find even more creative ways to keep busy. Your mind will spiral up and not down. Give your mind something powerful to focus on.

Shifting your thinking can help you transition into the type of thinking that will allow you to envision a new path for yourself and then work to achieve that change. To have more success in all areas of your life, you need to recognize that you and only you have the responsibility of choice — and to change your environment. You are the one that has to move your foot forward to take that step.

I can help you decide where you want to place your foot, but you need to be the one to take that step. As you create new roots for yourself, it will be easier to push forward. Recognize that you are teaching yourself a new skill, one that is going to require you to step outside of your comfort zone. Like any new skill, it might feel awkward at first, but over time that awkwardness will fade.

I want you to stop for a moment and think about the language you use when trying to do something new. There are phrases that you can use which will indicate how successful you can be. When you start with a negative mindset and speak negatively about what you are attempting, then you are likely to find yourself giving up if it is not successful on the first try.

Too often, people focus on what they are doing wrong or they ask "why questions." For example, "Why does this happen to me?" Notice when you shift your mindset and start to create new strategies and processes, you begin to look at what you are doing that is amazing. Then you might start asking yourself, "How do I focus on expanding that positive energy?" Positive thoughts and energy attract more positive thoughts and energy.

Now, shift that language to more positive language. Do you see the difference in how willing you are to keep going in the face of challenges? How you talk about something and what you focus on about that item or experience can help determine if you will be successful or not. When you say, "I can get into this," it is positive. When you say, "I won't be able to get this done," it is negative. Pay attention to what you say. It is very important. The point of new roots is that you are changing your focus and how you speak about the events in your life.

I want to push you to step outside of your comfort zone and think about how you talk to yourself and how you talk out loud to others. What are you truly ordering up on the menu of life? If you are not clear and using clear, positive language, you are probably going to continue to find your goals thwarted or the delivery being less than what you had hoped to achieve. You think you are ordering a 12-course meal, yet you get back liver stew.

After taking my four years of training, I realized that I now had a skill that would help me push forward in my life and to create an amazing future for myself. I know how to talk to my goal-getter, and the results have been incredible. I want you to have the same experience. By taking the time to look at your mental language, you can find the patterns or places where communication is breaking down and create new positive processes.

It is up to you to create new roots and allow yourself to be at peace with your past, just as it was up to me to do that for myself. Once you put all the pieces into place, then the possibilities are endless.

When you are defining your new roots, you need to have a laser focus on what you want. Distraction can keep you from achieving what you want. If you find that you are distracted, remember that you do not have to stay that way!

Part of my pushy training is about pushing you to move past those distractions and to regain your focus. You have control over your thoughts. Consider your thoughts as leaves on a running river. If you are standing on the bank of the river, then you will see those leaves floating passed you. Your thoughts are also moving at the speed of a river, so you need to decide which leaf to grab.

That is how you need to focus, simply by picking one positive thought or idea and then giving it your full attention. When you focus on a pattern of negative thoughts, then you are going to find that type of energy coming your way. However, when you immediately decide to focus on the positive, then you draw that positive energy towards yourself.

Here are just a few examples of the types of positive energy that you can create with your thoughts: love, understanding, and compassion. It is about flexibility to focus and also to dream and live in a creative space.

Now that you have an understanding of how you can control your thoughts, you can identify the patterns that could be obstacles in your life. The obstacles are a tapestry of limiting decisions, negative beliefs and values, to name a few. These drive you to take action or not. If your drive in the past has allowed you to coast, then we need to push the gas pedal. Change involves making the move to throw the bags out of the trunk, thus lightening your load. Then press the accelerator to the mat and take off!

Recap:

- Shift your thinking from the negative to the positive.
- Take control of your thoughts. You have the power!

- Create a laser focus on what you desire to achieve.

Now, I want to shift your focus to the last three elements I will be discussing in this chapter.

ELEMENT #3 - PURSUE YOUR DESIRES

Align your life and business to your desires. We have looked in detail at the root causes and received the learnings and released the negative emotions from the events. We have created new roots and realizations. You are thinking about things differently and in a new light. Now you may have determined what you want and may even have a vague idea of how you are going to get there.

You may find that, now, you are ready to focus on how you are going to achieve the life you desire or even to focus on the fact that such a life is possible. Remember, use direct and clear language with yourself and others that defines a specific path. If you don't do this you might not get what you expect, even though you followed the path. Your words and phrases need to be in alignment with the possibilities. The various parts of you need to be integrated, and then you need to decide on a clear path.

As you sharpen your definition of the life you desire, you give your mind something to work with. Start by asking great questions of yourself and others. Get curious about what you like and what you don't. When you work at home, which tasks tend to go quickly, and which ones tend to drag on and on?

Define your strengths and weaknesses. They can help you see what areas might be creating challenges in your life that you need to address. How can your strengths work more effectively for you? What might you need to go learn more about to turn your weaknesses into strengths?

One of the best ways to truly define the life that you desire is to visualize yourself in the life you want today as if you already have it. Write out in a journal that ideal and desired life. Give it as many details as possible. Include what it feels like, sounds like, smells like, and looks like. See yourself there and then describe that image. Act as if it is today you have what you want. I am sure that you might have done something similar in the past, but now that you have looked at root causes, it is time to do it again. What you focus on only gets bigger as you get accustomed to taking those massive actions! Focus on the desire.

One caution about focusing on your desire is to not stay in the future all the time. It is a beautiful dance to be able to be in the present most of the time and also focused on the future at times. It is about putting the desire in the future with you in the picture and then being in the present to complete the tasks.

It is also about fun. Being in the present is fun. I will straight out start belly laughing in the middle of something, and people say, "It is her laughing time." That laughing time is catchy though, and others soon start to laugh along. It is also my process for bringing me back into the present. I enjoy floating around in the future, sometimes too often. The action happens in the present.

You want to have everything you ever dreamed of in your life. You and I only get one chance at this life. What is holding you back? What are you going to do about it? Clearly, throughout our discussion, I have identified some root causes that you need to consider, as they could be blocks. However, I have also shared a few points to help you address them. Now I want to connect with you to help you to shift your thinking and keep going on the journey at my website, www.pushycoach.com.

Recap:
- Define your desires.

- Determine what is holding you back.
- Don't stay in the future, but keep a foot in the present.

ELEMENT #4 - ACTION

All that I have talked about throughout this chapter has led to this element, the one regarding action. Too many of us focus on the fear of a situation, and that keeps us from acting. However, when you focus on what you want — I mean laser focus — that fear will go away. You will move forward, despite the fear.

You must choose your mindset. Success is a decision. Not having success is a decision as well. A positive mindset takes work. It's like working a muscle. The more you go to the gym, the bigger the muscle. The more you focus on your positive mindset, the better the chance of getting that desire. You make the desire bigger and brighter, bigger and brighter.

When you learn the pattern of clear focus, then your vision gets bigger, clearer, and brighter. Focusing on the future and then acting on that vision means you are focusing on the future and not on the past. It is a sure sign that you are growing strong roots and are ready to move forward.

When you do make strides forward and an obstacle gets in your way, or you fail at something, it could be easy to decide to quit. A lot of people quit and tell themselves, "I guess it wasn't meant to be."

Keep your power and the ability that you have to be successful. If you are starting to do something that you have never done before, why would you expect not to have obstacles or that you might not have failures along the path to success? It is unrealistic to think that way.

Put positive processes in your mind every day. Give your mind exercise. Going back to the coach story, you recognize that coaches are consistently telling you new teachings and giving you more motivation — not once, consistently! Doing small things consistently is the key.

People get busy doing tasks that have nothing to do with their desire and then the day disappears — a week, a month, a year, ten years. Act now.

Additionally, it is critical to have a support team in place to help you as you transition to your shifted life. This is why I love setting up Mastermind groups. Masterminds are where like-minded people get together to work on a clear direction and get the wisdom and experience from the entire room, not just yours alone. Who is in your support team? Think about the people you rely on for advice, encouragement, and motivation. Are they providing that or are they bringing out the negative and showcasing a critical spirit?

Recognize that to build a positive support team, you need to be willing to be a positive support to others. That quality will draw people of like-mind to you. Do not be afraid to let go of the people that are limiting you, despite your efforts to be supportive of their dreams. Perhaps letting go of that relationship will make room for greater opportunities, including the chance to meet new people who can join your inner circle.

My point is that I know you are going to achieve great things. Do you know it? Once you do achieve them, it is important to celebrate and express gratitude to help keep those positive roots nourished.

Recap:
- Take the first step to create success.
- Build a support team.
- Be supportive of others, and it will return to you!

ELEMENT #5 - CELEBRATION AND GRATITUDE

Probably the best part of achieving anything in life is the satisfaction of knowing that you accomplished what you set out to create. That can be the push you need to start a new project or create a new chapter in another area of your life. I always believe in celebrating your successes, as it can be a true source of motivation and inspiration. However, celebrations do not have to be limited to times when you accomplish something or are successful in an effort. Find at least one thing to celebrate everyday!

When I do my talks, I ask the group if they have celebrated themselves that day? I always raise my hand. My hand is often the only hand raised.

Why is this the case? You are so good at being hard on yourself that you are not good at celebrating yourself and your accomplishments. Without your struggles and obstacles, then you would not be who you are. You are an amazing individual, especially because of your blemishes and scars. Your marks say who you are, and they make you the strong person you are. That is something to celebrate.

The point is that celebrating yourself is meant to push you forward to the next level and shift your thinking to bring you the life you desire. Part of that process involves being grateful for what you have achieved already. Gratitude is something that you can pass on to others, and it creates a positive energy that only grows.

Part of celebrating yourself involves exploring what you enjoy and trying new things. When you find fun things to do, then they keep you in a great state of mind. You have the choice to create your day your way, so why not start as soon as your eyes open! Starting this way could be the most comfortable and rewarding process of your day.

Recap:

- Celebrate what you have accomplished.
- Be grateful for your abilities.
- Explore new things and step outside of your comfort zone.

SHIFTING YOUR THOUGHTS STARTS NOW!

Here is a 10-minute process for you to begin shifting your thinking first thing in the morning. Do it consistently. Before even setting your feet on the ground.

This process is known as the "Push through to your purpose" process. It is given to you from the The Pushy Coach®. I created this so that people can shift their thinking even before they put their feet on the ground first thing in the morning. When does the mind start with its noise? Right — first thing! Beat your mind and put in the shift of positive energy before your feet hit the floor. You can do this process even before you are out of bed or while you are still stirring. I call this process the easiest process because you are still in bed. You can begin to build healthy roots for your amazing life from the comfort and warmth of your own bed.

1. Decide and choose this time to not only wake up physically and emotionally, choose to wake up consciously and to live on purpose.

2. Set an intention for your day. Intentions are critical for taking action. Some examples to get you started.

   a. I am open to new positive experiences today.

   b. I experience myself of service to others today.

    c. I am 100 percent present and aware with others today.

    d. I experience myself healthy, wealthy, and unconditionally happy today.

3. Say three to seven gratitude statements. What are you happy about? Some examples to get you started.

    a. I am grateful for the sun.

    b. I am grateful for my family and/or friends.

    c. I am grateful to have woken up this morning.

    d. I am grateful for the fresh air today.

4. Celebrate one success from the day before.

5. Say, "I like myself. This day is the best day ever!"

6. Visualize great things happening today. Get up you amazing person.

7. Repeat the process daily.

The secret is to focus on what you want. With these few new things to do, even before you get out of bed, you will be creating a great add-on to the success elements that you are already making a part of your life.

To do something different — to break through your comfort zone barrier — is part of living your desired life. When you get proactive to your outcomes and desires and less reactive to limiting decisions, beliefs, unaligned values, and more, then you can truly move your life onto the path that allows you to have an amazing life journey.

You can say you didn't know before, but now you do know. To live and to pursue your desired life is a choice you can make or not. Taking action is a responsibility. Consider yourself pushed. If you need a bigger push, then contact me at www.pushycoach.com or ask us about our 1-year "Shift to the Next Level" coaching package and also how to get the bonus 5-hour "Breakthrough Experience".

I believe in tearing out the old roots so much that I want to get you a fresh beginning by taking the "Breakthrough Experience" before starting your Next Level Coaching to get you to the next level in your life. In the Breakthrough Experience, you can learn to release root causes, and in the "Shift to the Next Level" coaching, you can lock in new roots to pursue your desired life with action. Take action and celebrate yourself and others with gratitude.

I appreciate you, and I thank you for taking the time to read through and learn about next level thinking. With you here, it also helps me move forward to a new way of thinking. When you think about it, there is always a next level, and we can do it together.

To learn more about Alana Leone,
please go to www.pushycoach.com

Step Into Greatness

LES BROWN

You have greatness within you. You can do more than you could ever imagine. The problem most people have is that they set a goal and then ask "how can I do it? I don't have the necessary skills or education or experience".

I know what that's like. I wasted 14 years on asking myself how I could be a motivational speaker. My mind focused on the negative—on the things that were in my way, rather than on the things that were not.

It's not what you don't have but what you think you need that keeps you from getting what you want from life. But, when the dream is big enough, the obstacles don't matter. You'll get there if you stay the course. Nothing can stop you but death itself.

Think about that last statement for a minute. There's nothing on this earth that can stop you from achieving what it is that you want. So, get out of your way, and quit sabotaging your dreams. Do everything in your power to make them happen—because you cannot fail!

They say the best way to die is with your loved ones gathered around your bed. But what if you were dying and it was the ideas you never acted upon, the gifts you never used and the dreams you never pursued, that were circled around your bed? Answer that question right now. Write down your answers. If you die this very moment what ideas, what gifts, what dreams will die with you?

Then say: I refuse to die an unlived life! You beat out 40 million sperm to get here, and you'll never have to face such odds again. Walk through the field of life and leave a trail behind.

One day, one of my rich friends brought my mother a new pair of shoes for me. Now, even though we weren't well off, I didn't want them; they were a size nine and I was a size nine and a half. My mother didn't listen and told my sister to go get some Vaseline, which she rubbed all over my feet. Then my mother had me put those shoes on, minding that I didn't scrunch down the heel. She had my sister run some water in the bathtub, and I was told to get in and walk around in the water. I said that my feet hurt. She just ignored me and asked about my day at school, how everything went and did I get into any fights? I knew what she was up to, that she was trying to distract me, so I said I had only gotten into three fights. After a while mother asked me if my feet still hurt. I admitted that the pain had indeed lessened. She kept me walking in that tub until I had a brand new pair of comfortable, size nine and a half shoes.

You see, once the leather in the shoes got wet, they stretched! And what you need to do is stretch a little. I believe that most people don't set high goals and miss them, but rather, they set lower goals and hit them and then they stay there, stuck on the side of the highway of life. When you're pursuing your greatness, you don't know what your limitations are, and you need to act like you don't have any. If you shoot for the moon and miss, you'll still be in the stars.

You also need coaching (a mentor). Why? There are times you, too, will find yourself parked on the side of the highway of life with no gas in the vehicle. What you need then is someone to stop and offer to pick up some gas down the road a ways and bring it back to you. That person is your coach. Yes, they are there for advice, but their main job is to help you through the difficulties that life throws at all of us.

Another reason for having a coach is that you can't see the picture when you're in the frame. In other words, he or she can often see where you are with a clarity and focus that's unavailable to you. They're not going to leave you parked along the road of life, nor are they going to allow you to be stuck in the moment like a photo in a frame.

And let's say you just can't see you're way forward. You don't believe it's possible. Sometimes you just have to believe in someone's belief in you. This could be your coach, a loved one or even a staunch friend. You need to hear them say you can do it, time and again. Because, after all, faith comes from hearing and hearing and hearing.

Look at it this way. Most people fail because of possibility blindness. They can't see what lies before them. There are always possibilities. Because of this, your dream is possible. You may fail often. In fact, I want you to say this: I will fail my way to success. Here is why.

I had a TV show that failed. I felt I had to go back to public speaking. I had failed, so I parked my car for ten years. Then I saw Dr. Wayne Dyer was still on PBS and I decided to call them. They said they would love to work with me and asked where I had been. I wasn't as good as I had been ten years before, as I was out of practice, but I still had to get back in the game. I was determined to drive on empty.

Listen to recordings, go to seminars, challenge yourself, and you'll begin to step into your greatness, you'll begin to fill yourself with the energy you need to climb to ever greater heights. Most people never attend a seminar. They won't invest money in books or audio programs. You put yourself in the top 5 percent just by making a different choice than the average person. This is called contrary thinking. It's a concept taken from the financial industry. One considers choosing the exact opposite behaviour of the average person as a way to get better than average results. You don't have to make the contrarian choice, but if you don't have anything to lose by going that road, why not consider the option?

Make your move before you're ready. Walk by faith not by sight and make sure you're happy doing it. If you can't be happy, what else is there? Helen Keller said, "Life is short, eat the dessert first."

What is faith? Many of us think of God when we think of faith. A different viewpoint claims that faith is a firm belief in something for which there is no proof. I would rather think of faith as something that is believed especially with strong conviction. It is this last definition I am referring to when I say walk by faith not by sight. Be happy and go forth with strong conviction that you are destined for greatness.

An important step on your way to greatness is to take the time to detoxify. You've got to look at the people in your life. What are they doing for you? Are they setting a pace that you can follow? If not, whose pace have you adjusted to? If you're the smartest in your group, find a new group.

Are the people in your life pulling you down or lifting you up? You know what to do, right? Banish the negative and stay with the positive; it's that simple. Dr. Norman Vincent Peale once said (when I was in the audience), "You are special. You have greatness within you, and you can do more than you could ever possibly imagine."

He overrode the inner conversations in my mind and reached the heart of me. He set me on fire. This is yet another reason for seeking out the help of a coach or mentor or other new people in your life. They can do what Dr. Peale did for me. They can set your passion free.

How important is it to have the right kind of person/people on your side? There was a study done that determined it takes 16 people saying you can do something to overcome one person who says you can't do something. That's right, one negative, unsupportive person can wipe out the work of 16 other supportive people. The message can't be any clearer than that.

Let's face the cold, hard truth: most people stay in park along the highway of life. They never feel the passion, the love for their fellow man, or for the work they do. They are stuck in the proverbial rut. What's the reason? There are many reasons, but only one common factor: fear — fear of change, fear of failure, fear of success, fear they may not be good enough, fear of competition, even fear of rejection.

"Rejection is a myth," says Jack Canfield, co-author of The Chicken Soup for the Soul series. "It's not like you get a slap in the face each time you are rejected." Why not take every "no" you receive as a vitamin, and every time you take one know you are another step closer to success.

You will win if you don't quit. Even a broken clock is right twice a day.

Professional baseball players, on average, get on base just three times out of every ten times they face the opposing pitcher. Even superstars fail half of the time they appear at the plate.

Top commissioned salespeople face similar odds. They make may make one sale from every three people they see, but it will have taken them between 75 and 100 telephone calls to make the 15 appointments they need to close their five sales for the week. And these are statistics for the elite. Most salespeople never reach these kinds of numbers.

People don't spend their lives working for just one company anymore. This means you must build up a set of skills and experiences that are portable. This can be done a number of ways, but my favourite approaches follow.

You must be willing to do the things others won't do in order to have tomorrow the things that others don't have. Provide more service than you get paid for. Set some high standards for yourself.

Begin each day with your most difficult task. The rest of the day will seem more enjoyable and a whole lot easier.

Someone needs help with a problem? Be the solution to that problem.

Also, find those tasks that are being consistently ignored and do them. You'll be surprised by the results. An acquaintance of mine used this approach at a number of entry-level positions and each time he quickly ended up being offered a position in management.

You must increase your energy. Kick it up a notch. We are spirits having a physical existence; let your spirit shine. Quit frittering away your energy. Use it to move you closer to the achievement of your dreams. Refuse to spend it on non-productive activities.

What do people say about you when you leave a room? Are you willing to take responsibility—to walk your talk. There is a terrible epidemic sweeping our nation, and it is the refusal to take responsibility for one's actions. Consider that at some point in any situation there will have been a moment where you could have done something to change the outcome. To that end you are responsible for what happened. It's a hard thing to accept, but it's true.

Life's hard. It was hard when I was told I had cancer. I had sunken into despair, and was hiding away in my study when my son came in. My son asked me if I was going to die. What could I do? I told him I was going to fight, even though I was scared. I also told him that I needed some help. Not because I was weak but because I wanted to stay strong. Keep asking until you get help. Don't stop until you get it.

A setback is the setup for a comeback. A setback is simply a misstep on the long road of success. It means nothing in the larger scheme of things. And, surprisingly, it sets you up for your next win. It tends to focus you and your energy on your immediate goals, paving the way for your next sprint, for your comeback.

It's worth it. Your dreams are worth the sacrifices you'll have to make to achieve them. Find five reasons that will make your dreams worth it for you. Say to yourself, I refuse to live an unlived life.

If you are casual about your dreams, you'll end up a casualty. You must be passionate about your dreams, living and breathing them throughout your days. You've got to be hungry! People who are hungry refuse to take no for an answer. Make NO your vitamin. Be Five Key Elements for Success. Be hungry.

Let me give you an example of what I mean by hungry …

I decided I wanted to become a disc jockey, so I went down to the local radio station and asked the manager, Mr. Milton "Butterball" Smith, if he had a job available for a disc jockey. He said he did not. The next day I went back, and Mr. Smith asked "Weren't you here yesterday?" I explained that I was just checking to see if anyone was sick or had died. He responded by telling me not to come back again. Day three, I went back again—with the same story. Mr. Smith told me to get out of there. I came back the fourth day and gave Mr. Smith my story one more time. He was so beside himself that he told me to get him a cup of coffee. I said, "Yes, sir!" That's how I became the errand boy.

While working as an errand boy at the station, I took every opportunity to hang out with the deejays and to observe them working. After I had taught myself how to run the control room, it was just a matter of biding my time.

Then one day an opportunity presented itself. One of the disc jockeys by the name of Rockin' Roger was drinking heavily while he was on the air. It was a Saturday afternoon. And there I was, the only one there.

I watched him through the control-room window. I walked back and forth in front of that window like a cat watching a mouse, saying "Drink, Rock, Drink!" I was young. I was ready. And I was hungry.

Pretty soon, the phone rang. It was the station manager. He said, "Les, this is Mr. Klein."

I said, "Yes, I know."

He said, "Rock can't finish his program."

I said, "Yes sir, I know."

He said, "Would you call one of the other disc jockeys to fill in?"

I said, "Yes sir, I sure will, sir."

And when he hung up, I said, "Now he must think I'm crazy." I called up my mama and my girlfriend, Cassandra, and I told them, "Ya'll go out on the front porch and turn up the radio, I'M ABOUT TO COME ON THE AIR!"

I waited 15 or 20 minutes and called the station manager back. I said, "Mr. Klein, I can't find NOBODY!"

He said, "Young boy, do you know how to work the controls?"

I said, "Yes, sir."

He said, "Go in there, but don't say anything. Hear me?"

I said, "Yes, sir."

I couldn't wait to get old Rock out of the way. I went in there, took my seat behind that turntable, flipped on the microphone and let 'er rip.

"Look out, this is me, LB., triple P. Les Brown your platter-playin' papa. There were none before me and there will be none after me, therefore that makes me the one and only. Young and single and love to mingle, certified, bona fide and indubitably qualified to bring you satisfaction and a whole lot of action. Look out baby, I'm your LOVE man."

I WAS HUNGRY!

During my adult life I've been a deejay, a radio station manager, a Democrat in the Ohio Legislature, a minister, a TV personality, an author and a public speaker, but I've always looked after what I valued most—my mother. What I want for her is one of my dreams, one of my goals.

My life has been a true testament to the power of positive thinking and the infinite human potential. I was born in an abandoned building on a floor in Liberty City, a low-income section of Miami, Florida, and adopted at six weeks of age by Mrs. Mamie Brown, a 38-year-old single woman, cafeteria cook and domestic worker. She had very little education or financial means, but a very big heart and the desire to care for myself and my twin brother. I call myself Mrs. Mamie Brown's Baby Boy and I say that all that I am and all that I ever hoped to be, I owe to my mother.

My determination and persistence in searching for ways to help my mother overcome poverty and developing my philosophy to do whatever it takes to achieve success led me to become a distinguished authority on harnessing human potential and success. That philosophy is best expressed by the following …

> "If you want a thing bad enough to go out and fight for it,
> to work day and night for it,
> to give up your time, your peace and your sleep for it…
> if all that you dream and scheme is about it,
> and life seems useless and worthless without it…
> if you gladly sweat for it and fret for it and plan for it
> and lose all your terror of the opposition for it…
> if you simply go after that thing you want
> with all of your capacity, strength and sagacity,
> faith, hope and confidence and stern pertinacity…
> if neither cold, poverty, famine, nor gout,
> sickness nor pain, of body and brain,
> can keep you away from the thing that you want…
> if dogged and grim you beseech and beset it,
> with the help of God, you will get it!"

Branding
Small Business

RAYMOND AARON

Branding is an incredibly important tool for creating and building your business. Large companies have been benefiting from branding ever since people first started selling things to other people. Branding made those businesses big.

If you're a small business owner, you probably imagine that small companies are different and don't need branding as much as large companies do. Not true. The truth is small businesses need branding just as much, if not more, than large companies.

Perhaps you've thought about branding, but assumed you'd need millions of dollars to do it properly, or that branding is just the same thing as marketing. Nothing could be further from the truth.

Marketing is the engine of your company's success. Branding is the fuel in that engine.

In the old days, salespeople were a big part of the selling process. They recommended one product over another and laid out the reasons why it was better. Salespeople had credibility because they knew about all the products, and customers often took the advice they had to offer.

Today, consumers control the buying process. They shop in big box stores, super-sized supermarkets, and over the Internet — where there are no salespeople. Buyers now get online and gather information beforehand. They learn about all the products available and look to see if there really is any difference between them. Consumers also read reviews and check social media to see if both the company and the product are reputable. In other words, they want to know what the brand is all about.

The way of commerce used to be: "Nothing happens till something is sold." Today it's: "Nothing happens till something is branded!"

DEFINING A BRAND

A brand is a proper name that stands for something. It lives in the consumer's mind, has positive or negative characteristics, and invokes a feeling or an image. In short, it's a person's perception of a product or a company.

When all goes well, consumers associate the same characteristics with a brand that the company talks about in its advertising, public relations, marketing and sales materials. Of course, when a product doesn't live up to what the company says about it, the brand gets a bad reputation. On the other hand, if a product or service over-delivers on the promises made, the brand can become a superstar.

RECOGNIZING BRANDING AND ITS CHARACTERISTICS

Branding is the science and art of making something that isn't unique, unique. Branding in the marketplace is the same as branding on a ranch. On a ranch, ranchers use branding to differentiate their cattle from every other rancher's cattle (because all cattle look pretty much the same). In the marketplace, branding is what makes a product stand out in a crowd of similar products. The right branding gets you noticed, remembered and sold — or perhaps I should say bought, because today it is all about buying, not selling.

There are four main characteristics of branding that make it an integral part of the marketing and purchasing process.

1. Branding makes you trustworthy and known

Branding makes a product more special than other products. With branding, a normal, everyday product has a personality, and a first and last name, and people know who you are.

In today's marketplace, most products are, more or less, just like their competition. Toilet paper is toilet paper, milk is milk, and a grocery store by any other name is still a grocery store. However, branding takes a product and makes it unique. For example, high-quality drinking water is available from just about every tap in the Western world and it's free, but people pay good money for it when it comes in a bottle. Branding takes bottled water and makes Evian.

Furthermore, every aspect of your brand gives potential customers a feeling or comfort level that they associate with you. The more powerful and positive that feeling is, the more easily and more frequently they will want to do business with you and, indeed, will do business with you.

2. Branding differentiates you from others

Strong branding makes you better than your competition, and makes your product name memorable and easy to remember. Even if your product is absolutely the same as every other product like it, branding makes it special. Branding makes it the first product a consumer thinks about when deciding to make a purchase.

Branding also makes a product seem popular. Everyone knows about it, which implicitly says people like it. And, if people like it, it must be good.

3. Branding makes you worth more money

The stronger your branding is, the more likely people are willing to spend that little bit extra because they believe you, your product, your service, or your business are worth it. They may say they won't, but they will. They do it all the time.

For example, a one-pound box of Godiva chocolates costs about $40; the same weight of Hershey's Kisses costs about $4. The quality of the chocolate isn't ten times greater. The reason people buy Godiva is that the brand Godiva means "gift" whereas the brand Hershey means "snack". Gifts obviously cost more than snacks.

4. Branding pre-sells your product

In the buying age, people most often make the decision on which products to pick up before they walk into the store. The stronger the branding, the more likely people are to think in terms of your product rather than the product category. For example, people are as likely, maybe even more likely, to add Hellmann's to the shopping list as they are to write down simply mayo. The same is true for soda, ketchup, and many other products with successful, strong branding.

Plus, as soon as a shopper gets to the shelf, branding can provide a quick reminder of what products to grab in a few ways:

- An icon or logo
- A specific color
- An audio icon

BRANDING IN A SMALL BUSINESS

Big companies spend millions of dollars on advertising, marketing, and public relations (PR) to build recognition of a new product name. They get their selling messages out to the public using television, radio, magazines, and the Internet. They can even throw money at damage control when necessary. The strategies for branding are the same in a small business, but the scale, costs, and a few of the tactics change.

Make your brand name work harder

The name of a small business can mean everything in terms of branding. Your brand name needs to work harder for your business than you do. It's the first thing a prospective customer sees, and it is how they will remember you. A brand name has to be memorable when spoken, and focused in its meaning. If the name doesn't represent what consumers believe about a product and the company that makes it, then that brand will fail.

In building your product's reputation and image, less is often significantly more. Make sure the name you choose immediately gives a sense of what you do.

Large corporations have millions of dollars to take a meaningless brand name and make it stand for something. Small businesses don't, so use words that really mean something. Strive for something interesting and be right on point. You don't need to be boring.

Plumbers, for example, would do well setting themselves apart with names like "The On-Time Plumber" or "24/7 Plumbing". The same is true for electricians, IT providers, or even marketing consultants. Plenty of other types of business are so general in nature they just don't work hard enough in a business or product name.

Even the playing field: The Net

The Internet has leveled the playing field for small businesses like nothing else. You can use the Internet in several ways to market your brand:

Website: Developing and maintaining a website is easier than ever. Anyone can find your business regardless of its size.

Social Media: Facebook and Twitter can promote your brand in a cost-effective manner.

BUILDING YOUR BRAND WITH THE BRANDING LADDER

Even if you do everything perfectly the first time (and I don't know anyone who does), branding takes time. How much time isn't just up to you, but you can speed things along by understanding the different levels of branding, as well as the business and marketing strategies that can get you to the top.

Introducing the Branding Ladder

Moving through the levels of branding is like climbing a ladder to the top of the marketplace. The Branding Ladder has five distinct rungs and, unlike stairs, you can't take them two at a time. You have to take them in order, and some businesses spend more time on each rung than others.

You can also think of the Branding Ladder in terms of a scale from zero to ten. Everyone starts at zero. If you properly climb the ladder, you can end up at 12 out of 10. The Branding Ladder below shows a special rung at the top of the ladder that can take your business over the top. The following section explains the Branding Ladder and how your small business can move up it.

THE BRANDING LADDER	
Brand Advocacy	12/10
Brand Insistence	10/10
Brand Preference	3/10
Brand Awareness	1/10
Brand Absence	0/10

Rung 1: Living in the void

Your business, in fact every business, starts at the bottom rung, which is called brand absence, meaning you have no brand whatsoever except your own name. On a scale of one to ten, brand absence is, of course, zero. That's the worst place to live and obviously the most difficult entrepreneurially. The good news is that the only way is up.

Ninety-seven percent of businesses live on this rung of the Branding Ladder. They earn far less than they want to earn, far less than they should earn, and far less than they would earn if they did exactly the same work under a real brand.

Rung 2: Achieving awareness

Brand awareness is a good first step up the ladder to the second rung. Actually, it's really good, especially because 97 percent of businesses never get there. You want people to be aware of you. When person A speaks to person B and says, "Have you heard of "The 24/7 Plumber?" You want the answer to be "yes".

On that scale of one to ten, however, brand awareness is only a one. It's better than nothing, but not that much better. Although people know of your brand, being aware doesn't mean that they are interested in buying it. Coca Cola drinkers know about Pepsi, but they don't drink it.

Rung 3: Becoming the preferred brand

Getting to the third rung, brand preference, is definitely a real step up. This rung means that people prefer to use your product or service rather than that of your competition. They believe there is a real difference between you and others, and you're their first choice. This rung is a crucial branding stage for parity products, such as bottled water and breakfast cereals, not to mention plumbers, electricians, lawyers, and all the others. Brand preference is clearly better than brand awareness, but it's less than halfway up the ladder.

Car rental companies represent a perfect example of why brand preference may not be enough. When someone lands at an airport and needs to rent a car on the spot, he or she may go straight to the preferred rental counter. If that company has a car available, it's a sale. However, if all the cars for that company have been rented, the person will move to the next rental kiosk without much thought, because one rental car is just as good as another.

Exerting Brand Preference needs to be easy and convenient

If all you have is brand preference, your business is on shaky ground and you can lose business for the feeblest of reasons. Very few people go to a second or third supermarket just to find their favorite brand of bottled water. Similarly, a shopper may prefer one store over another but, if both stores sell the same products, he or she will often go to the closest store even if it is not the better liked one. The reason for staying nearby does not need to be a dramatic one — the shopper may simply be tired, on a tight schedule, or not in the mood to travel.

Rung 4: Making it you and only you

When your customers are so committed to your product or service that they won't accept a substitute, you have reached the fourth rung of the Branding Ladder. All companies strive to reach this place, called brand insistence.

Brand insistence means that someone's experience with a product in terms of performance, durability, customer service, and image has been sufficiently exceptional. As a result, the product has earned an incredible level of loyalty. If the product isn't available where the customer is, he or she will literally not buy something else. Rather, the person will look for the preferred product elsewhere. Can you imagine what a fabulous place this is for a company to be? Brand insistence is the best of the best, the perfect ten out of ten, the whole ball of wax.

Apple is a perfect example of brand insistence

Apple users don't just think, they know in their heads and hearts, that anything made by Apple is technologically-advanced, user-friendly, and just all-around superior. Committed to everything Apple, Mac users won't even entertain the thought that a PC may have positive attributes.

Apple people love everything about their Macs, iPads, iPhones, the Mac stores and all those apps. When the company introduces a new product, many of its brand-insistent fans actually wait in line overnight to be one of the first to have it. Steve Jobs is one of their idols.

Considering one big potential problem

Unfortunately, you can lose brand insistence much more quickly than you can achieve it. Brand-insistent customers have such high expectations that they can be disillusioned or disappointed by just one bad product experience. You also have to consistently reinforce the positives because insistence can fade over time. Even someone who has bought and re-bought a specific brand of car for the last 20 years can decide it's just time for a change. That's how fickle the world is.

At ten out of ten, brand insistence may seem like the top rung of the ladder, but it's not. One rung is actually better, and it involves getting your brand-insistent customers to keep polishing your brand for you.

Rung 5: Getting customers to do the work for you

Brand advocacy is the highest rung on the ladder. It's better than ten out of ten because you have customers who are so happy with your product that they want everyone to know about it and use it. Think of them as uber-fans. Not only do they recommend you to friends and family, they also practically shout your praises from the rooftops, interrupt conversations among strangers to give their opinion, and tell everyone they meet how fantastic you are. Most companies can only aspire to this level of customer satisfaction. Apple is one of the few large corporations in recent history that has brand advocates all over the world.

- Brand advocacy does the following five extraordinary things for your company. Brand advocacy:

- Provides a level of visibility that you couldn't pay for if you tried. Brand advocates are so enthusiastic they talk about you all the time, and reach people in ways general media and public relations can't. You get great visibility because they make sure people actually listen.

- Delivers free advertising and public relations. Companies love the extra super-positive messaging, all for free.

- Affords a level of credibility that literally can't be bought. Brand advocates are more than just walking testimonials. They are living proof that you are the best.

- Provides pre-sold prospective customers. Advocate recommendations carry so much weight that they are worth much more than plain referrals. They deliver customers ready and committed to purchasing your product or service.

- Increases profits exponentially. Brand advocates are money-making machines for your business because they increase sales and decrease marketing costs.

For these reasons, brand advocacy is 12 out of 10!!

BRANDING YOURSELF: HOW TO DO SO IN FOUR EASY WAYS

If you're interested in branding your product or company, you may not be sure where to begin. The good news: I'm here to help. You can brand in many ways, but here I pare it down to four ways to help you start:

Branding by association

This way involves hanging out with and being seen with people who are very much higher than you in your particular niche.

Branding by achievement

This way repurposes your previous achievements.

Branding by testimonial

This way makes use of the testimonials that you receive but have likely never used.

Branding by WOW

A WOW is the pleasantly unexpected, the equivalent of going the extra mile. The easiest and most certain way to WOW people is to tell them that you've written a book. To discover how you can write a book of own, go to www.BrandingSmallBusinessForDummies.com.

Sex, Love and Relationships

DR. JOHN GRAY

Just as great sex is important to lasting love, good health is important to sex and relationships. About 12 years ago, I cured myself of early stage Parkinson's disease. The doctors were amazed, but my wife was even more amazed. She noted that our relationship and sex life had become dramatically better. It turns out that the natural supplements I used to reverse Parkinson's can also make you more attentive and loving in your relationship. At that point, I realized that good relationship skills alone were not enough to sustain love and passion for a lifetime.

I shared many insights gained from my 40 years' experience as a marriage counselor and coach in *Men Are From Mars, Women Are From Venus*. And while my insights go a long way towards helping men and women understand and support each other, good communication skills alone are not always enough. For better relationships, we not only need to be healthy, but we must also experience optimum brain function.

If you are tired, depressed, anxious, not sleeping well, or in pain, then certainly romantic feelings will become a thing of the past. My recovery from Parkinson's revealed to me the profound connection between the quality of our health and our relationships. This insight has motivated me, over the past twelve years, to research the secrets of optimum health as a foundation for lasting love.

These are health secrets that are generally not explored in medical school. In medical school, doctors are indoctrinated into the culture of examining the symptoms, identifying the sickness, and prescribing a drug to treat that sickness. They learn very little about how to be healthy or to sustain successful relationships.

There are no university courses entitled "Better Nutrition For Better Sex". Drugs sometimes save lives, but they also have negative side effects that do little to preserve the passion in a relationship. Ideally, drugs should be used as a last resort and 90 % of our health plan should be drug free. From this perspective, the heath care crisis, as well as our high rate of divorce in America, is indirectly caused by our dependence on doctors and prescription drugs.

Most people have not even considered that taking prescribed drugs (even for the small stuff) can weaken their relationships, which in turn makes them more vulnerable to more disease. For example, if you are feeling depressed or anxious, a drug may numb your pain, but it does nothing to help you correct the cause of your problem. It can even prevent you from feeling your natural motivation to get the emotional support you need. In a variety of ways, our common health complaints are all expressions of two major conditions: our lack of education to identify and support unmet gender-specific emotional needs; and our lack of education to identify and support unmet gender-specific nutritional needs.

With an understanding of natural solutions that have been around for thousands of years, drugs are not needed to treat many common complaints. Some symptoms like low energy, weight gain, allergies, hormonal imbalance, mood swings, poor sleep, indigestion, lack of focus, ADD and ADHD, procrastination, low motivation, memory loss, decreased libido, PMS, vaginal dryness, muscle and joint pain, or the lack of passion in life and/or our relationships can be treated drug-free. By using drugs (even over-the-counter drugs) to treat these common complaints, our bodies and relationships are weakened, making us more vulnerable to bigger and more costly health challenges like cancer, diabetes, heart disease, auto-immune disease, dementia, and Alzheimer's. In simple terms, by handling the easy stuff (the common complaints) without doctors and drugs, we can protect ourselves from the big stuff (cancer, heart disease, dementia, etc.) We can be healthy and also enjoy lasting love and passion in our personal lives.

Even if you are taking anti-depressants or hormone replacement therapy, sometimes all it takes to stop treating the symptom is to directly handle the cause. With specific mineral orotates (something most people have never heard of) or omega three oil from the brains of salmon, your stress levels immediately drop and you begin to feel happy and in love again.

For every health challenge, we have explored the effects on our relationships, with as well as natural remedies that can sometimes produce immediate positive results. You can find these natural solutions to common health complaints for free at my website: www.MarsVenus.com.

What they don't teach in medical school is how to be healthy and happy without the use of drugs or hormone replacement. By refusing drugs and taking responsibility for your health, a wealth of new possibilities can become available to you. We are designed to be healthy and happy, and it is within our reach if we commit to increasing our knowledge.

New research regarding the brain differences in men and women reveals how specific nutritional supplements, combined with gender-specific relationship and self-nurturing skills, can stimulate the hormones of health, happiness and increased energy. Over the past 10 years in my healing center in California, I witnessed how natural solutions coupled with gender-specific relationship skills could solve our common health complaints without drugs. By addressing these common complaints without prescribed drugs, not only do we feel better, but our relationships have the potential to improve dramatically.

Ultimately the cause of all our common complaints is higher stress levels. Researchers around the world all agree that chronic stress levels in our bodies provide a basis for any and all disease to take hold. An easy and quick solution for lowering our stress reactions is specific nutritional support combined with gender-smart relationship skills. Extra nutritional support is needed because stress depletes the body very quickly of essential nutrients. When a car engine is running more quickly, it uses fuel more quickly. When we are stressed, we need both extra nutrients and extra emotional support. Understanding what we need to take and where to get it requires education. Every week day at www.MarsVenus.com I have a live daily show where I freely answer questions and provide this much-needed new gender-specific insight.

At www.MarsVenus.com, we are happy to share what we have learned for creating healthy bodies and positive relationships. You can find a host of natural solutions for common complaints and feel confident that you have the power to feel fully alive with an abundance of energy and positive feelings that will enrich all your relationships.

Never Give Up!

My Journey to Purpose

VIVIAN STARK

NEVER GIVE UP: GROWTH AND SUCCESS COME IN INCREMENTS, NOT LEAPS

My desire is to encourage you with my life story. I have spent my life learning and improving myself, and I am thrilled to share what I have learned with you. Today I am living my definition of success. I have said NO TO THE PITY PARTY! Personal growth and development are a daily diet staple, and have fueled me in my business and entrepreneurial successes.

I wake up every day, knowing I am living my life with purpose, knowing I am the kind of person I always wanted to be. I have faced many challenges; my story has failures as well as successes. But I have learned that setbacks are

51

only a part of the story; they are not the whole story. The story keeps going as long as you keep trying. You can choose to quit and make the story end in failure or dissatisfaction, or you can choose to keep trying and make your story what you want it to be.

Never give up. Success and growth do not come in leaps, they come in increments. The challenges will keep coming at you and sometimes it feels like two steps forward, one step back. But remember you did have those steps forward and you will again – if you never give up. You can choose to be overcome by dreck that life throws at you, or you can open your eyes to the love and opportunity that are always there too. You can have the life you want if you never, never, never give up on what is important – You.

IT IS YOUR LIFE - LIVE IT YOUR WAY

My life is my own for the making, but I did not always know this. I lived a very sheltered life as a child, fiercely protected by my overbearing Greek parents. I was not allowed to do the 'normal' girl things, like have sleepovers or join the Girl Guides to be a Brownie. When I was older I was not allowed to date for fear of gossip within my community. My parents lived in fear of the unknown. I lived in fear of being reprimanded if I disobeyed.

Despite my fear, insecurity, and extremely introverted personality, I pushed myself to exert my independence and fulfill certain goals that I set out for myself. From a very young age, I felt that I always needed to prove myself. To prove that I was pretty enough, smart enough, or even good enough. I worked tirelessly to achieve my dreams, never sharing them with anyone for fear of being ridiculed.

I began pursuing my goals as a young teen who wanted to fit in. I lived in an affluent area of Vancouver and always felt out of place. I did not have all the cool clothes that everyone else had, so I worked with my brother as a gardener cutting grass for one of my dad's clients. I saved my money and bought the clothes I wanted so that I would 'fit in' with the crowd. Despite this, I never felt that I fit in with other kids.

I was a rather "ugly duckling" as a younger girl, with a massive overbite and awkward shyness about me. After having braces, I felt my "ugly" stage was behind me and I decided to take a modeling class over several weeks one summer when I was in high school. My parents did not support me in this decision, so I chose to pay for it myself. The modeling class cost $800. I worked at Zellers for $3.00/hour. I persevered and saved enough money to pay for the class.

It turns out that the modeling class was just what I needed. I learned how to carry myself and exude confidence. After finishing the class, I took several modeling jobs and had many successes in my short modeling career. I made the cover of the then prestigious Back to School catalog for Eaton's Department Store, along with several other fun and exciting modeling adventures.

My modeling highlight and a fond memory was when I was hired for a ski catalog. (They wanted a curvy model. Who knew that sometimes it pays to not be super skinny!) We were taken up to the top of Blackcomb Mountain by helicopter before the official ski season opening. I remember having to jump out of the helicopter into three feet of snow because the helipad was snow-covered, and the helicopter could not land. I was paid $850 per day for three days. It was a dream come true. I felt validated.

When I was nineteen I began dating a handsome Greek guy I met at a wedding. Before I knew it, his parents and my parents got together and began planning our wedding. I literally cannot remember him actually asking me to marry him. How sad is that? Some time before our wedding I found out that he was into drugs and was still seeing his ex-girlfriend. I broke up with him and cancelled the wedding.

To escape well-meaning friends and relatives, I took an extended holiday to Greece where I could recover from the breakup. Armed with my modeling composite cards and my lovely, fashionable clothes, I hoped to land some modeling jobs while I was there. Instead, I met another handsome Greek guy who was smooth and charming. He swept me off my feet.

In classic old-school Greek fashion, my mom flew to Greece to check him out and determine whether he was a suitable partner for me. Like I said, I lived a sheltered life. She approved and, after a civil wedding in Canada, I moved to Greece to start my life with my new husband.

The first thing he did when we settled in to our home was give away all my beloved clothes. He proceeded to tell me what I could and could not do, where I could and could not go, and how I had to act. He, like my parents, was consumed with what other people thought of him and now me. I was terrified. What had I done?

I realized very quickly I had made a huge mistake and wanted to leave him and go back to Canada. To my surprise, I was already pregnant. Too embarrassed to tell anyone my sad state of affairs, I stayed in Greece. I had made an agreement with my husband that our children would be born in Canada. I did not want to risk my children having to go to the army if they were boys. After my first son was born, I returned to Greece.

When I became pregnant with my second son, I decided to leave Greece, not to return. I told my husband I was going back to Canada and he could come with me or not. He chose to move to Canada with me, but we broke up after a few years. Our marriage was just not meant to be, but I was blessed with two healthy, adorable and rambunctious boys that I loved so much.

Once divorced, my husband went back to Greece to avoid paying child support and to be near his momma, so she could pamper and take care of him. (It's a Greek thing. He was a huge momma's boy. Never again.) I was determined that my two boys would never be momma's boys!

THE SETBACK IS NOT THE END OF THE STORY PUSH YOURSELF TO YOUR NEXT GREAT CHAPTER

For the next few years, I lived in low-income housing while raising my boys and working at Woodward's department store. Then, I left my job at Woodward's and began a career in banking. I started out on the front lines working as a teller. After six weeks I was promoted to the prestigious side counter position. Within a year I was promoted again to managing tens of millions of dollars of lawyers' trust funds in an exclusive, independent position.

I was always pushing myself to be better, to do more, be more, have more so I could give more. I wanted to improve myself and my income to support my family. I had an internal drive to never give up. I wanted to prove everyone wrong. I would make it. I could do this! During these years I learned to appreciate life's lessons and gifts and I continued to grow.

Ten years after my first marriage, I married a second time. I became pregnant soon after our wedding in Hawaii but spent most of my time during our marriage being neglected by my husband. As soon as my daughter was born, I no longer existed in his eyes. I later found out that my husband had a girlfriend before, during, and after our entire marriage. He worked with her; she was married, too, and the four of us occasionally hung out together as couples. Needless to say, the marriage did not last, but I would not change a thing as I have my beautiful daughter from that relationship.

I spent the next years relentlessly trying to find my passion. I worked in banking, direct sales, office supplies, a genealogical search company, and as a sales manager for a roofing distribution company. I also went to night school while working full-time and raising my kids, to get my diploma in International Trade. Additionally, I began a calling card company in Santiago, Chile that I launched at the Canada/Chile Trade Mission in 2003.

OPPORTUNITY KEEPS KNOCKING, SO OPEN THE DOOR!

I was very proud of the calling card company. It was a crazy dream, but I wanted to make it happen. Recognizing a huge opportunity, I wanted to offer an affordable service that we took for granted in Canada. The large telecommunications companies had a very different view on my entry to the marketplace and I was forced out of business when they pressured my distribution channel to drop me. Unfortunately, my venture was short-lived after significant effort and money had been invested. I planned to travel back to Chile to negotiate a deal with another distributor when I was rear-ended in a car accident and suffered severe whiplash, leaving me unable to travel. I had to move on from this company but by this time I knew it was not the end. I knew other opportunities would come my way.

By 2007, I was working for a computer company selling proprietary software and hardware for restaurants. My expertise in sales and customer service had grown significantly by then. I had come a long way from the introverted little Greek girl who thought she was not good enough. With perseverance, training, and a belief in myself I had become a great salesperson.

I loved working with customers and was enjoying my new career when I began having severe migraines regularly. I was also having issues with my sinuses. I thought I probably had a severe sinus infection, but my nose and upper gums were numb, which was troubling.

That August was one big headache, literally. I had eight migraines that month and each one put me down for two to five days. I went to the doctor and had several tests run, including a CT scan. After the CT scan doctors finally determined the cause of my sinus trouble and migraines.

I will never forget that day. The doctor's office called and scheduled me for a 7:00 PM appointment. The doctor came in and told me that I had a brain tumor and that she was very sorry, but she did not know whether it was benign or malignant. She had not consulted a neurologist before meeting with me. I drove home in a state of shock and called my mom to tell her the news.

I learned that I had a meningioma, a benign brain tumor. After an MRI, I learned it measured 3.3 x 3.4 x 4.4 cm, was in my right frontal lobe, and had probably been growing for twenty or thirty years. Only recently had it grown large enough to begin causing migraines, sinus pain, and facial numbness.

Within a month I would be having major brain surgery to remove the tumor. Oddly enough, I was not scared until the day of the surgery, when it really sunk in. I had been told that the tumor was in an excellent location for surgery and that I would not need chemo or radiation afterwards. The tumor was not going to kill me. But with any surgery there is always a risk.

I do not remember much that happened the first week or so post-surgery. When I really came around and began noticing things, the first thing that caught my attention was that I was having significant vision problems. The brain surgeon had touched a nerve in my right eye, causing fourth nerve palsy. I always had this weird talent to do crazy thing with my eyes and move them independently, but this was something I could not control. I had severe double vision. I could only see straight when I looked through a very narrow view if I tilted my chin down. And I could not look to my left at all. When I tried, I lost all focus and control of my eyes.

This condition is similar to a child having a wandering eye. Actually, I had to be seen at Vancouver Children's Hospital to have my condition monitored. This was a very challenging time for me. It was one of the worst times of my life. I had so much stress and anxiety wondering if my vision would be like this forever. My head was permanently disfigured, leaving my self-esteem at an all-time low. My jaw was so stiff from surgery that I could barely open my mouth to eat. I was house-bound, and unable to walk up or down stairs without assistance. I could not read or watch TV to occupy myself because I was constantly dizzy. Every negative thought you could possibly imagine ran through my mind thousands of times each day. I wish I had known then what I know now about keeping a positive mindset, the healing powers of affirmations, an attitude of gratitude, and the law of attraction.

I cannot stress enough how important it is to reach out to family and friends to help you during a medical crisis (or any crisis, for that matter). Having people who love you to support you is so important. Being the independent person that I am, I did not ask for much help. Silly me. Stupid me, actually. I did not want to worry my kids any more than they already were. My mother was such an angel. She lived nearby and prepared meals for us, but for the most part, I was alone in my thoughts in a very dark place.

About five weeks into my recovery, I met someone online. Bored out of my mind, I had gone on a dating site, half-blind, looking for strangers to converse with me. Talk about being desperate! For our first meeting, I rode the bus to downtown Vancouver where we met for a drink. He must have thought I was rather forward on a first date when I grabbed his arm to walk up a few stairs. Little did he know that I grabbed his arm so that I would not fall flat on my face.

We hit it off and developed a relationship. He picked me up every day for several weeks and took me out on his random errands just to get me out of the house. Sometimes we would just hang out. At first, I only told him that I'd had a recent eye surgery. Eventually I told him the extent of the surgery. He was also having some challenges in his life, so it was wonderful to be able to help each other. I cannot tell you what a godsend he was for me. He came into my life exactly when I needed him, and I am forever grateful for what he did for me.

Worried about losing my job, I returned to work twelve weeks post-surgery. I was worried about paying my bills and the mortgage on the house I had recently purchased. I needed the money, or so I thought. In hindsight, that was the worst decision I could have made. I suffered with migraines and vision issues for several weeks before the universe decided I'd had enough. All of the senior managers, including me, were laid off from our jobs. It was the biggest blessing.

I did not work for two years. It was a very trying time. The line of credit was on a steady increase as the months went by, but I needed to heal. My vision took over a year to somewhat normalize, and the severe numbness in my face post surgery lasted for several years.

During this period, I had a lot of time to think. My surgery was a life-changing experience. I could have died. I decided to take on a totally different view on life from this time forward. From this point on, any time an opportunity presented itself I was going to take it.

DEFINE YOUR WORK AND WHAT YOU NEED

Knowing that after all my health problems I would need a job that allowed me to make my health a priority, I decided to choose a job that would work for me rather than choosing to work for the job. I started slowly by taking a 100% sales commission, part-time position that allowed me to work as much or as little as I wanted.

I told my bosses about my medical condition, and that I was not sure how I would respond to being back to work. My boss told me that as long as I was meeting or exceeding my quotas that he would not micromanage me. I would be allowed to do my own thing, which was perfect for me. For some this would be a scary venture to undertake, but I was up for the challenge.

I pushed myself by working long hours, often answering customer emails at 6:00 AM before I went to work and again well into the evening. I needed to build up my customer base and wanted to ensure they were well taken care of. Within less than six months I was working full-time and making a full-time income. I was back!

After working for this company for about four years, a couple of millennials were hired into the mix, and that changed everything for me. I was working independently with little interaction with my bosses for the most part and the millennials were cc'ing him on every email they sent. This is when my interest in generational differences in the workplace was first piqued.

Although I enjoyed the work and my co-workers, my bosses were a different story. My work environment left much to be desired. Receiving year-end bonuses based on sales is a standard practice in the world of sales. When I did not receive a bonus at the end of 2013 because my boss said I was "already making too much money," I decided to look at other business opportunities. Forever the entrepreneur!

I continued working my sales job while seeking other opportunities. I joined an Australian direct sales company and quickly rose to the top of their company, becoming one of their top 20 earners out of 20,000 consultants. I had 1,700 consultants on my team and was the only director in North America. I earned free trips to Australia, Dubai, Aruba, Florence, Manchester, Dallas, and Los Angeles. I finally left my sales job in 2016 to pursue my new business venture full-time.

DREAM BIG AND HELP OTHERS DREAM TOO

I LOVED working with my team. Coaching and mentoring were my passion. In October 2016, I attended a One Day to Greatness seminar with Jack Canfield in Kamloops, BC. After a brief conversation with Jack, I decided to take his Train the Trainer course to become a certified Success Principles Trainer. The intention was to share this new knowledge with my team. I had found purpose and passion in supporting others to build successful teams. I felt fulfilled when I saw their self-esteem and confidence grow. They were conquering their fears and winning!

Unfortunately, I had to resign from the direct sales company in February 2017 when they started having issues with production and delivery. Later that year the company declared bankruptcy. I went through a lot of stress, anxiety, and loss of sleep. Panic attacks became the daily norm for me. I had known the CEO for over eighteen years and was completely in the dark about the state of the company. My team was upset and blaming me. I received a constant stream of Facebook messages and harassing emails. The downfall of the company was out of my control, so I had to bow out. But this was not my first time at the rodeo. I knew that my story did not stop here if I chose to keep trying.

I met someone in late 2016 who introduced me to an opportunity to speak and train businesses on generational differences in the workplace. I was fascinated by this as I saw the struggles my own millennial children were having at work. I look back now at the communication challenges that existed in my previous jobs and wish I knew then how the different generations think and process information. I wanted to more closely understand their environment and what I could do to help. It made perfect sense that bridging the generation gap would improve productivity, communication, collaboration, and make for a happier, more cohesive work environment.

I now know that the behaviors, attitudes, beliefs, experiences, and influences during an individual's formative years really shape who they are and how they behave in all areas of their lives. I was excited about my new-found knowledge, and planned to launch my speaking business by mid-2017.

I hired an image consultant to come to my home and do a complete wardrobe change to prepare me for my speaking career. Having someone go through my wardrobe and tell me to get rid of most of it was a very difficult experience. There were a few tears. I must have attachment issues! I eventually embraced the change and spent thousands of dollars on a new wardrobe to complete my new look.

Then, as luck would have it, I broke a veneer on my front tooth. No big deal, I thought. I had been through this before and would just have it replaced.

This was the beginning of my dental nightmare. From May 31, 2017 through December 21, 2017, I had twenty-six dental appointments to fix my front tooth. I began lisping and developed what doctors believe is a stress-related condition. I lost the saliva in my mouth, had burning in my throat from acid reflux brought on by stress, my voice was constantly hoarse, and I spent several months waking up with panic attacks. I never knew from one to day to the next if I would have a voice or not, so I had to put everything on hold.

I saw every doctor and specialist I believed might be able to help me. I was taking six pills a day to help with my various symptoms. I hated this! I needed to feel better; I needed to heal my body naturally. I would not stop until I got the answers I needed. I moved away from traditional medicine, stopped taking all my medications, and began incorporating EFT (Emotional Freedom Technique), also known as Tapping, Reiki, and Bioenergy work, to heal my body.

Eventually, my body and voice were getting to the point where I could speak relatively well, I decided to move forward with the training business. I hired a business coach to get me on the right track, mentally and physically. He helped me tremendously during a very difficult time. I also attended Raymond Aaron's Speaker and Communication Workshop, which totally changed my training and speaking style. It gave me the confidence I was lacking and sent me on a whole new trajectory for my business. I began my own company, Gen-Connect Training in early 2018. It has been an amazing ride. I am much more at peace and ready for the next stage in my life.

LIVING IN THE POSITIVE HAS MADE MY LIFE

Although I have been blessed with many struggles, I have also enjoyed many successes. I have experienced relationships that did not work out, work and business challenges, worries when raising three children as a single parent, medical challenges, and many dreams and goals that seemed impossible. The one thing I always knew for sure was that if I gave up and wallowed in self-pity, I would be letting myself and my children down. That was not an option. Success was the only acceptable outcome.

I wanted to show my children what a strong, self-sufficient and resourceful mother I could be, and that they could always rely on me. I wanted to set an example and prove to myself and my children that I could provide for us no matter what. I am very proud of the amazing people my children have become; they are strong, independent, kind, respectful, and loving. This is the true meaning of success for me. Out of all the things I have accomplished thus far, they are my crowning glory.

FIVE STRATEGIES FOR A SUCCESSFUL LIFE

1) **Always have a positive mindset.** This is a crucial component. Before you get into the power of a positive mindset and the law of attraction, spend some time listening to what you are currently telling yourself. Check in with yourself. What is going on with you? We constantly speak to ourselves with an inner voice which is sometimes quietly whispering and sometimes yelling. Once you have spent a few days noticing how you speak to yourself, you may not like it very much; after all, you are your own worst critic. Be accountable for how you speak to yourself. Never fear, you have the power to change that inner voice!

Do you believe you are the product of everything that has happened to you in your life? Your inner voice may try to convince you that you are a victim of your circumstances and your past. Reflect and acknowledge the things that have happened to you and where you are now. Then prepare to move past them.

2) Shift your mindset using the law of attraction. You can influence things around you so that things happen FOR you rather than TO you. The universal principle of the law of attraction is that 'like attracts like.' The law of attraction manifests through your thoughts by drawing to you not only thoughts and ideas that are alike, but also people who think like you, along with corresponding situations and possibilities. It is the magnetic power of the universe which draws similar energies to each other.

The law of attraction is already working in your life, intentional or not. If you have a negative mindset, many unpleasant or unwanted things are probably happening in your life, and you may see negative things happening all around you. Think back to how you speak to yourself. Be mindful of your thoughts and that inner voice. Begin to think positively.

Along with thinking positively, begin to intentionally think and feel the things that you would like to have in your life. The most common things people desire are love, a career, good relationships, health, and wealth. Visualize a mental image of what you want to achieve. Repeat positive, affirming statements to create and bring into your life what you visualize or repeat in your mind. In other words, use the power of your thoughts and words.

Imagine that what you desire is already a part of your life. Acknowledge it with each of your five senses, to the extent that you can. Spend time imagining your life once you have acquired what it is that you want. Write out your affirmations and read them aloud at least once daily. You will begin to draw them to you when you act as though you already have what it is that you want. Persistence is key!

3) Take calculated risks. Do you encourage yourself to stay where you are and play it safe? Safe can be dangerous. I encourage you to take calculated risks. If you do not try new things you will never know how far you can go. When opportunities present themselves, jump on them. It may be your one and only chance. Push yourself and do not take no for an answer. Keep digging until you find the answer you want.

Quitting is always an option. Well, it is an option for those who are content living a mediocre life. Quitting is an option unless you want to live an amazing life with a purpose. If you want to live the life of your dreams, you must not give up. Do not give up and never stop learning. If you continue to learn, you will continue to grow both personally and professionally.

4) Appreciate all of life's lessons and gifts with an attitude of gratitude. Learn and grow from your failures. Let life's challenges teach you to persevere even when all you want to do is give up. Remind yourself that the only outcome you will accept is success.

5) NEVER Give Up. We all face adversities and challenges in life. It takes character, drive, and a positive mindset to persevere, overcome, and excel in life. The only person who can stop you from achieving your goals is you. If I can do it, so can you. Go for it!

Do you, your team, or organization want to be inspired to change your future and find your purpose?

Do you want to learn how mastering the Five Strategies for A Success Life can empower you in both your personal and professional career?

Do you want to say "NO TO THE PITY PARTY" and achieve the life you truly desire?

Vivian Stark is an inspirational speaker and corporate trainer living in Vancouver, B.C. Canada, whose captivating story will inspire you to live the life you want if you never, never, never give up on what's important – You.

As a generational and workplace effectiveness expert, Vivian's career centers around helping others work in a more collaborative and cohesive work environment. Her focus on engagement and accountability both in and outside of the workplace mirrors her personal belief of how you must take 100% responsibility in all areas of your life. Learn how giving up blaming, complaining and excuse making can lead you to live a life filled with peace, happiness and personal fulfillment.

To learn how you can incorporate her knowledge and expertise into your life and business with ease and confidence, reach out to Vivian at www.gen-connect.ca. Vivian is available for private or corporate speaking engagements.

Big Business Selling Strategies For Small Business Growth

GARY THOMPSON

T he vast majority of small business owners, whether they offer a service or make and sell a product, are good at what they do. But, being wonderful at something doesn't automatically translate into being wonderful at selling or marketing it. Most small business owners lack the skills they need to manage successfully and grow their businesses, which is probably why so many of them fail during their first few years.

There are two key issues that are problematic. The first is that today, many small business owners come out of corporate environments. After 15, 18, or 20 years, they decide it's time to quit the proverbial rat race and start doing something they actually like, hopefully, love to do. If you're one of them, you know that it's scary at first. It's hard to get a new business off the ground, especially if you are used to being part of a team. In a small business, you're largely on your own, with no accounting, marketing, or sales department for support. It's all up to you.

So, you start wearing about 12 different hats, doing all kinds of tasks on your own, from cleaning the floors in the morning to shutting everything up in the evening. Instead of spending your day doing the one thing you started a business to do, you move from chore to chore. Plus, when you are that busy doing, you never have the time to think about marketing and growing your business.

Often, the hardest task you take on is salesperson because, at some point in the conversation, you have to talk about money. It's not necessarily difficult to share your passion for the business or talk about the wonderful things that your product or service does for the customer, but closing the sale and discussing the price can be truly uncomfortable. Even someone who has been in sales at another company can still feel some level of guilt about asking for an order at the retail price when it's for themselves. And that's a huge impediment to being an independent business owner. It's crucial to learn how to sell your product or service for what it — and you — are worth.

It's not a matter of garnering selling expertise or knowing what you know. Unfortunately, knowing isn't enough. You must also believe it, and believe in yourself. You need to understand and respect your own worth, as well as the worth of your product or service. If you can learn to sell without feeling like you are begging for money, then you can grow your business as opposed to just running that business.

Of course, first, you have to get to the point when you are running your company, not just working in it. Once you start generating more income by closing the sale more often, you will have the funds to start hiring people to handle the tasks that are diverting you from being a real owner. It's not as easy as sounds because, once you eliminate the classic excuse for not delegating ("I'd love to hire somebody, but I can't afford to"), it is time to face the underlying reasons why letting go of the little things is so difficult.

In many ways, this is more a personal decision than a business one in that the business reason is obvious: your time is worth more than what you would have to pay others to do the bookkeeping and buy the stationery supplies. The hard part is making the psychological shift that will allow you to trust other people to do as good a job as you can. If you can get over that hump just once, it will become easier each time you do it.

Coaching both corporate and small business clients has helped me codify a process for overcoming these all too common personal issues that keep people from realizing their full business or career potential. It starts with developing, cultivating and maintaining your sense of business-related worth, and then delivering the story of that worth in a compelling and believable manner. This chapter provides an overview of the five key things on which you will need to focus.

FIVE POWERFUL ELEMENTS TO LONG TERM BUSINESS GROWTH

1. Craft Your Story

The most important thing you need is your story, which means understanding who you are, what you stand for, why you are doing what you are doing and with whom you are looking to work. The key is focusing on the why. You may already be familiar with the best example of building and maintaining a compelling story, but it bears repeating because the Apple case study is excellent at making the point.

The company has done an extraordinary job, and it isn't necessarily because their products are any better than anybody else's. The company has an ethos, an approach that involves going well beyond the status quo, especially as it relates to customer service. In developing its story, Apple has given itself a huge advantage over other corporate cultures, one that draws people to the company. That advantage is the why, as in better customer service is the reason why to buy an Apple instead of a computer from one of its competitors.

A lot of small business owners lose or forget their why when they get involved in the day-to-day running of their companies. They forget why they are doing it, whatever it is, because they spend all their time actually doing it.

2. Create an Experience

Remembering your why helps you understand, envision and create the experiences your clients are going to enjoy from their interaction with you. Your product may work better than others of its kind, your customer service may be superior, the sales experience easier and so on.

3. Build a Narrative

Your narrative is a personalized version of what marketing experts call a positioning statement. It tells much of your story in that it puts forth a picture of who you are and what you're doing, and summarizes the benefits of being one of your clients. Since you are the one who will be telling your narrative, you need to feel comfortable with the words and the thoughts behind those words. You need to know and feel that you are telling the truth. It's important that the narrative you put out makes sure you're seen as the person you want to be, and that your customers' actual experiences support your narrative.

4. Be Selective

Trying to appeal to any and everyone is a marketing strategy that may work for large corporations with products that actually appeal to everyone, but it is a tragic mistake for small business owners. Think of it in terms of someone going door-to-door, trying to sell magazine subscriptions. That's basically what you're doing when you sit at your desk with a phone in your hand, calling a list of cold prospects. The same is true when you take the networking route, drop leaflets or run blanket advertising. The process is archaic and makes for extremely hard, time-consuming work. Worse still, it is soul destroying.

There are better ways of finding clients and customers, but they only work when marketing and sales genuinely work together. The concept of true cooperation between the two may feel foreign if you come out of the corporate world, where marketing and sales are separate entities somewhat in competition with each other. In fact, and the way it should work, marketing generates leads, and the salespeople convert them.

Your marketing efforts are to there to help people raise their hands and say "Yes, I'd like to talk to you." When there has been prior interaction with a lead who has self-identified themselves as interested in your product, the conversation is totally different than it is during a cold call. There is much less pressure put on you to justify the cost of your product, and that lessens or removes the guilt about discussing money. Distancing yourself from lead generation is also essential to better managing your time and your efforts. The time to step into the process is when a viable lead has been identified and engaged.

5. Know Your Numbers

When marketing and selling are working in tandem, you can trace the conversion process and its associated costs, from reaching someone and getting them to self-identify through to the final sale and the amount of that sale. Tracking these figures along with the lifetime value of a customer will allow you to determine how much it costs to acquire a new client or customer, as well as the value of an average customer. This will allow you to confidently set your marketing budget for attracting new customers and long-term growth.

IT'S EASIER WITH HELP

As discussed earlier in this chapter, most small business owners already find themselves trying to do it all on their own. Delegating some or all of the everyday activities can be a huge help in freeing up your time to begin rethinking the marketing and selling plan for your own company.

However, if you are like most people, you will soon see that there is a big difference between knowing what to do, understanding what activities go into doing it, and actually doing it on a regular basis. Everything in life takes a bit of a learning curve and enough practice on a regular basis so that you feel comfortable doing things in a different way. The process is the same for any new beneficial habit; you need to keep feeding it and watering it, much in the way you would water and feed a sprout until it becomes a healthy, growing plant.

The good news is that you don't have to go through the process alone. A good advisor can guide you through the learning curve and help you manage the time commitment involved so that you don't end up putting too much pressure on yourself. An advisor can also help you hold yourself accountable in terms of getting things accomplished. That's something that just about everyone struggles with in most areas of life, but especially so in business — and even more so when you are running and trying to grow your own business. Perhaps most importantly, a good advisor knows how to help you work through any of the "I'm not good enough" feelings and insecurities that affect just about everyone at some time.

If you would like to learn more about what goes into taking these five steps at Gary Thompson's Workshops, please visit www.ThatTallGuy.com

Nobody Got Time For That!

The Ultimate Guide For Smart Money Management

URSULA GARRETT

S ave, save, save! That's all you hear from family, friends and the media. You are strongly encouraged to save, but how are you supposed to save with a low-paying job, high student loan debt, and the rising cost of housing? Something has got to give – and it's usually not you giving to your savings account. Who has time to be broke when you are young and just want to have fun and enjoy your life? I'll tell you who – nobody. Nobody has got time for that, especially you!

Finances absolutely play a huge part in your life choices and opportunities. Money issues consume chunks of your brain power every day. Think of how many times money (or a lack of it) factors into your decisions throughout your fast-paced day. For instance, you schedule a date on Tinder, buy movie tickets on Fandango and make dinner reservation using Open Table, and you haven't even gotten out of bed yet to start your day. You can do this if you have money in your bank account or power (available credit) on your credit card. Yes, either method of payment will get you what you want right now – one is a smart choice and the other, not so much. You must make smart choices regularly, there is no getting around it.

Size does matter, especially when it refers to your bank account. I want you to recognize that money underwrites the type of life you live and the lack of it means you're not living the life you want to be living. You are forced to make hard choices about what you can afford or what you have to give up. Having limited options make you feel as if your life is less than it could be. Smart money management is the key to your financial goals and personal goals aligning.

Once you recognize that the choices you make with your finances are either limiting your options or providing you opportunities, you can start being more proactive with your finances. First, it is important for you to understand how easy it is to handle your personal business, so you can create real changes that will significantly impact your life.

Two of my five daughters are about the same age, 26 (not twins just a blended family). Throughout their lives, they have taken different paths and made different choices. They are in their mid-twenties now and both spend more than they should, however, one is contributing to a retirement plan and has money go directly from her paycheck into a savings account. The other one lives paycheck to paycheck, has no retirement savings, no personal savings, and is regularly subsidized by her parents. Three guesses which one has more opportunities to live the life she wants, and the first two guesses don't count. While they each had similar opportunities, their individual choices have dictated their current circumstances.

"I am not a product of my circumstances. I am a product of my decisions."

- Stephen Covey

It's a bit of a mystery why you make some of the decisions you make and that's especially true when it comes to your finances. I can tell you from experience that a crystal ball, mesmerizing though it may be, is not where you will find those answers. How often have you made poor financial choices in the moment, only to later regret them and wonder how you got into this situation again? Well, I'm here to tell you that it doesn't matter how or why, what matters is what you do to fix it and make sure it never happens again.

If you have ever paid attention to political elections, then you know how easily you can be fooled by your assumptions, fears and false intuitions. I say this to help you understand that listening to others' opinions about what you should do won't help you reach your goals. Making a plan and following through will.

Which is why I find it useful to understand some principle concepts when you make decisions about money. This is besides, of course, the regular practices of following a budget, saving, investing and avoiding most kinds of debt, factors that I will discuss as part of the steps for smart money management.

These four concepts are the foundation you need for your decision-making process when you are creating your budget or making the decisions about those investments and savings plans. They need to factor into all your financial decisions, because they will help keep you from sabotaging your financial stability.

1) OPPORTUNITY COSTS

No matter what you do or the opportunities that you pursue, there is always going to be a cost. You have to give something to get something. Nothing in life is free. Individually, we get to decide what we are willing to give in exchange. In some circumstances, the price is simply too high, or the payoff is too low to make the deal or take the chance. That threshold is different for everyone and is based on your values.

For example, deciding whether or not to pursue higher education is a decision you make based on your priorities, which could include your financials, your time, and your perception of the value of higher education. Pursuing an advanced degree may take years -- are you willing to put in that amount of time? It could involve giving up other opportunities to finish your degree, but at the same time, the network you build could allow you access to individuals who can create even greater career opportunities in the future. Many individuals choose their university based on the alumni and the type of network they can access for mentors.

Additionally, there is the debt that often comes with pursuing higher education. Are you willing to put yourself into that kind of debt, the type of debt that will take years to pay off? Many individuals see their degree as a doorway to career advancement in a specific field or as a way to pursue the type of work that they are passionate about. For them, the cost of the degree in terms of finances and time is worth it, because they see that degree as an investment in their long-term financial future.

Those two daughters I mentioned earlier, one went to college and has a degree in business and some student loan debt. The other worked part-time jobs and traveled to visit friends she met on the internet. One daughter wanted a college degree and was willing to sacrifice four years of her life, accumulate debt (she considered it as an investment) and forego immediate travel opportunities. The other daughter thought that price was too high. This isn't a matter of right or wrong but a matter of what you are willing to give to get what you want. Here is a general rule of thumb: The bigger the opportunity, the greater the cost or sacrifice to achieve it.

Every decision that you make has all those considerations and it is up to you to give them all a voice before you make your decision. At the same time, your priorities need to guide those smaller financial decisions that we all make throughout the day. Many of your long-term goals are going to be impacted by your short-term decisions. Therefore, giving yourself guidelines for daily spending based on your priorities will help you to reach those goals. Still, not everything can be quantified in terms of your return on investment, as I will explore next.

2) SUNK COSTS

What is sunk cost? This is money you can't get back -- a non-refundable airline ticket, for example. There are certain expenses that you will have throughout your life that are not going to bring a tangible return on investment. In fact, they are likely going to result in nothing more than an enjoyable experience or a pleasant memory. It can be easy to get into a mindset that has you spending far beyond what you may have budgeted or prioritized because you value the experience, but it can put you in a financial bind later. The idea here is that you need to keep sunk costs in proper perspective. It's easy to start thinking, "Well, I've already spent $100, so what's another $25?" My mother always told me not to throw good money after bad. She taught me to understand the concept of sunk costs long before I took a business class. You have got to be willing to walk away sometimes and keep the money in your pocket for other investment opportunities.

Once something is paid for, and cannot be refunded, it shouldn't impact your future financial decisions. It is a "sunk" cost, i.e. water under the bridge, and no matter what you do in the future you won't ever get it back. Therefore, you can't allow yourself to get hung up on the moments where you spent money in a way that didn't fall into your overall financial plan. In the end, you have to accept that sunk costs are going to happen and make your peace with them. Recognize that you will buy emotionally and defend rationally, even if that might not always be wise. There are costs that are simply not recoupable.

Regrets over sunk costs can make it harder to move forward, leaving you vulnerable to make other choices that you may not have otherwise made. Do not allow yourself to fall into the downward spiral. Negative thoughts often breed more negative thoughts, especially if you continue to dwell on them. The same can be said for financial decisions. When you focus on your bad financial decisions, you may find yourself repeating them, because that is your focus.

It is important to keep yourself focused on ways to improve your financial decisions and keep them in line with your financial plan. Yes, you might regret a decision, but make the conscious choice not to dwell on it. Instead, learn from it and move forward. Life, especially when it comes to finances, is a series of learning experiences. The better you are at accepting the lessons, the better decisions you will be able to make in the future. I find inspiration and humor in the lyrics of one of my favorite songs by Chumbawamba, "I get knocked down, but I get up again, you're never gonna keep me down."

Now that you have that mindset (and that song stuck in your head), you can keep yourself from making financial decisions based on your sunk costs and focus on maximizing your earnings. That starts by focusing on finding the right investments for you. With that in mind, let's talk about the Rule of 72.

3) QUICK INTEREST CALCULATIONS USING THE RULE OF 72

One of your biggest concerns about an investment should be, "What am I going to get out of this?" While you wouldn't want to ask that of a date, it's perfectly acceptable, in fact it's expected, to ask that of a potential investment. All of us want a way to determine the upside of a financial opportunity. Now there are several ways to analyze a financial investment, but it often comes down to how long it will take for an investment to pay off. Want to double your holdings? The Rule of 72 can tell you how long it will take, based on the specific interest rate. Just divide 72 by the interest rate to learn how long it will take to double your initial investment.

For example, if you are looking at an investment with an interest rate of 6 percent, then 72 divided by 6 gets you 12 years. You can then take that information and use it to determine if that timeframe will work with your overall financial plan. Granted, you may find that other factors will play a part in determining your return as well, but it is important to have an idea of what you can expect before you put money into an investment.

This is a rough estimate, of course, but it's pretty effective. Recognize that you might find that a return is going to take significantly longer to make you money. So even if you find it an interesting opportunity, you may opt to not invest in order to take advantage of a different opportunity that will give you a faster return on your money.

In fact, you can also turn the equation around to determine the interest rate you are looking at if someone promises to double your returns in a set amount of time. Twice as much money in 12 years? Divide 72 by 12 and you get an interest rate of 6 percent. This rule lets you evaluate investment opportunities quickly and decide where to put your money in a way that will help you to grow your investments to meet long-term financial goals.

Keep in mind, future earnings are not something that you can count on, so how you use the dollars that you have now are going to have greater weight than potential earnings. You know that old saying, "Don't count your chickens before the eggs hatch."

4) THE TIME VALUE OF MONEY

According to this concept, a dollar you receive today is worth more than a dollar you will get tomorrow. You will have opportunity to invest that dollar immediately and begin earning more revenue from it (and also avoid losing value because of inflation).

It is important to recognize that money from your investments needs to be put to work. Don't be quick to spend it. Making frivolous or useless purchases means you are making a choice to spend on meaningless things and activities and in doing so, you are draining your ability to invest and grow. Focus on how you can essentially create a chain of investments, all working to grow an income stream for you to use in retirement or even for a big purchase that is part of your financial plan (think a house or car). Growth is a long-term process and it is imperative that you do make the time for it.

When you are waiting for an investment to pay off, then you are waiting for your money to work for you. One of the ways that you can save money is by limiting your interest payments. When you are making money from investments, which is then reinvested, you create an income stream that can allow you to pay cash for items, or put down a larger down payment, thus helping to reduce those interest payments, or eliminate them altogether.

Again, this helps you make certain calls about your purchases -- and your income. It's the old "one bird in the hand is worth two in a bush" theory in action for your wallet.

These four concepts have served me well over the years. Now let's focus in on the five steps that will help you to remain financially sound as you invest and grow your income to meet your financial goals.

WHY MONEY MATTERS

Before I talk about the steps, I want you to understand that money has a place and purpose in your life. Whatever adventures or experiences you want to have, you are going to need money to do it. That money is also going to be a key part of fulfilling your life's purpose, simply because money is a resource that can help you get things done. Regardless of if your goal in life is to have a non-profit that helps others or to create a company to bring a product or process to market, the truth is that money will be a resource that you need.

Since you and I can agree on that, let's start talking about your financial goals by first talking about your life goals.

STEP 1 - BUDGETING: YOUR PERSONAL BUSINESS PLAN

You have goals you want to accomplish, experience, and create in this life. This is simply a reality we all share. By defining your goals, you are able to determine what financial moves are necessary to achieve them. Too often, personal goals are overlooked or under-appreciated when creating a financial plan. Your personal goals and your financial plan need to be in sync for you to be successful at achieving either one.

For instance, if you know that your financial plan is going to allow you to achieve your personal goals, then it will help you maintain the excitement and vision you have for your life. This knowledge will help keep up the momentum during tough times or difficult circumstances when you are making sacrifices.

Budgeting should be the first part of your financial plan, because it will show the money you have coming in and going out. Once you understand your cash flow, then you have all the information you need to make a sound financial plan. Your budget will allow you to make good choices about how you want to use your money and where you can make changes in your spending habits to align your personal goals with your financial goals.

As part of that budgeting process, you need to look at the choices you make on a daily basis. Consider that if you take out that Tinder date on Saturday night maybe you can't afford to play golf on Sunday. If you really want to golf, then maybe you have to Netflix and chill with $1 bottles of beer or a $7 bottle of wine and takeout pizza instead of your dinner and a movie date. We all have to make choices. Just make sure your choices are good choices. You may find that you are sabotaging yourself by the financial decisions you make every day.

The good news is that you don't have to try to figure out a budget on your own or hire a professional to do it for you. All you need is that device that sometimes acts as another appendage – your cell phone. Yes, there is another reason that your cell phone is your best friend because there's an app for that (for budgeting, that is). Actually, there are several apps for that, you just have to choose the one that works best for you.

I use Mint to track my personal bank accounts, credit cards, investments and bills – it creates a budget based on my income and expenses and reminds me when I have a payment due date. I love that my whole financial life is accessible in one place and that I can monitor activity at a glance. One of my daughters uses Clarity Money, which has similar features plus the added benefit of helping to cancel unwanted subscriptions. With an app, you won't have to wonder if you are spending too much money shopping or eating out, you can see it in full color. Knowledge is power, and this knowledge can be used to change your spending behavior to match your financial goals.

For instance, think about that $5 cup of coffee you stop to buy every morning to start your day. That money falls into the sunk costs pot, because you are not getting that money back and it is not working for you. Imagine how much money you could save if you took that $5 per day for a year and saved or invested it – you would have more than $1,825. Going back to those two daughters of mine, one likes to buy and play internet games, a lot – can you guess which one? I'll tell you it's not the one that uses Clarity Money. If you are having trouble saving to meet your long-term goals, then it might be worth exploring using an app to help you get control of your spending.

It is not about giving up your lifestyle, but making your lifestyle adhere to your financial priorities, instead of letting your lifestyle dictate your priorities. Everyone has time to know their money.

Part of achieving any financial goal is to create a nest egg of funds to work with, which serves as a basis for your investment portfolio. Using your budget, you can designate a specific percentage to go into your savings.

STEP 2 – SAVING

The point of saving is to create a financial resource that you can use to build your income streams. These income streams can be diversified, but the point is that saving has to be a priority in order to improve your financial situation and allow you to reach your goals. Here are just a few reasons why saving is important.

1. You have a nest egg for emergencies. Time and time again, financial emergencies have sunk individuals who appear to be doing well, simply because they had nothing to fall back on. Once it happens, they have a financial issue, one that can have a ripple effect across other areas of their lives. Point blank, having an emergency, such as an unexpected car repair or house repair, should not financially sink you. Experts recommend that your savings for emergency needs to cover six months of your living expenses. Once you reach that goal, keep saving a set amount to grow your emergency fund. If you have to use some of it for an emergency, then replace it as soon as possible.

2. You can save for larger purchases. You know that paying cash for items can save you money in the long run, because you won't pay interest on top of the purchase cost. When you designate savings for specific

purchases, it allows you to reach your financial goals without acquiring payments. Plus, once you make that big purchase, you can start saving for the next big item or event.

3. You can save to invest to build income streams. Once you have achieved your emergency savings goal, start building a savings that is specifically for investments. These funds should not be used for any other purpose, allowing you to adjust the rate of return to meet your goals.

Clearly, saving is important because it gives you a stepping stone to meet your financial needs and personal dreams. Now, I want to transition to the exploring the possibilities that you can create with a savings that was started for investing.

STEP 3 – INVESTING

When you reach the point that you have started an investment savings account, you have plenty of opportunities. From stocks and bonds to direct investing in a business, you have multiple ways to grow your investment dollars. That being said, it is important to choose investments that fall in line with your goals and your risk tolerance level.

For instance, if you are at the beginning of your career, you might find yourself more inclined to look for high return, risky investments. Why? Many of those who are younger see time on their side and recognize that they have time to recover from a loss. Alternately, as you reach specific benchmarks or get closer to achieving your financial goals, you will start to make less risky investments.

Another potential scenario is that you are planning to get married or start a family, in which case, you might be more concerned with the risk of losing the primary financial provider. In a case like this, you may be more interested in investing in a disability or life insurance policy or even starting a college fund. After all, not all investments are created equal.

Where you are in your life can play a large part in what type of investments you choose to take on. Additionally, you might take on investments that are less time-consuming because they give you the ability to do more of what you enjoy. On the other hand, you might want to be more hands-on in your investments, so that may be a factor in the types of investments you choose.

Your investment plan should be personalized to you and designed to meet your needs. I want you to recognize that working with a financial advisor can help you to determine the best investments for you.

Many of the individuals I work with even consider investing in themselves, which means starting their own business. If you want to explore your entrepreneurial spirit, that can be a great way to invest and see your returns grow, using your investment dollars and sweat equity. Again, I encourage you to put any investment up against your financial plan. Ask yourself the hard questions about whether it will work towards accomplishing your goals. Doing so is critical to keeping you focused and on the path to achieving both your financial and personal goals. Just keep in mind that it takes time to grow and any time frames set by you can be changed, especially if the situation changes.

STEP 4 – AVOIDING MOST KINDS OF DEBT

Debt can drown you financially and make it difficult for you to achieve your financial goals. When you look at your budget, do you see areas where you are spending money on payments regularly? That is money which is not being used to create income streams or to reach your financial goals.

Be picky when you are choosing to take on debt. I recommend that you only finance things that will bring in money or pay for themselves. It's okay to finance your education because you expect your education to yield you a higher paying career. Do not finance your vacation because you will have nothing but memories to show for it. You can pay for your business advertising with a credit card but not your groceries. Avoid running up your credit cards, leaving yourself strapped with payments. The interest payments can quickly exceed your budget and be a drain. Use the cash in your bank account to pay for your living expenses because the interest on credit cards is usually greater than the interest you earn on money deposited in the bank.

Some debt can be beneficial and preferable because it shares the risk. I am talking about debt that involves investing. For instance, if you are building a real estate portfolio of rentals and you have $100,000 to invest, you might find that you choose to split that $100,000 into down payments for five properties instead of just buying one for $100,000. The reason is that you can increase your cash flow across five properties and they can also cover their own overhead. In the meantime, you are creating equity that you can tap into later to purchase more properties. The point is that you want to use your investment cash to maximize your income opportunities. Do not limit yourself because you want to avoid all debt – some debt can be good.

When weighing your debt options, be sure to look at interest rates. Do not feel as if you are limited to one lender or one financing option. Shop around and make sure that you get the lowest possible rate for your debt with the best payment plan to meet your investment needs. Also, make sure that any investment purchased with debt is going to have a positive cash flow. Some investments may not have a positive cash flow initially but will overtime as the debt is paid down. For other investments, it is the value which grows over time that offsets the lack of a positive cash flow.

Again, it is important to work with a professional who can help you determine what types of debt you want to take on regarding your investments and what debt you want to avoid.

In the end, this step is mostly focused on helping you to avoid debt that drains you financially, without giving you any type of return. Think about the cost of those daily coffees. The focus of this step needs to be on defining the lifestyle you want and then investing in order to be able to afford it. If you opt to live a lifestyle that drains your investments, you could be shortchanging yourself for the future, thus limiting your ability to reach your dreams.

STEP 5 – EVALUATE AND ASSESS: ONGOING PROCESS

I call this step, "the shit happens" part of your plan. Yes, it would be nice if life happened exactly as we planned it, but real life is no fairy tale. The reality is that you made a plan based on the life you wanted to live and all the messy stuff that got in your way is why you had contingency plans, emergency funds and cushions built into your plan. Shit happens, and you deal. You deal by adapting to your new situation. Update your plan as if it is a living, breathing organism.

For instance, you had an accident that kept you from working for six months. That would be both physically and financially draining. This is only a temporary setback. Now you need to reset your goals to achieve your plans, because you may need to focus on rebuilding instead of growth. Still, the point is to make adjustments that help you achieve your goals, thus not allowing the circumstances to overwhelm you and derail your finances permanently.

This need to make adjustments also applies to your investments. I recommend at least once per quarter that you review your investments to make sure they are performing as expected. You don't want to waste your resources on underperforming investments.

Are there areas you might want to expand even further, or do you need to eliminate some investments because they no longer fit your financial goals? Doing these reviews regularly can help you to keep your financial life on track with your personal life. When the two are in sync, then you will find that your life continues to improve. This harmony makes it possible to achieve what you want, no matter the setbacks you might occasionally encounter.

Keep in mind that evaluating and assessing will always be ongoing processes. The fluidity of life is that you can create plans, but events may alter those plans or even offer you new opportunities and experiences that you might not have even considered.

It is important to keep your mind open, both to new investments and to new experiences and opportunities in your personal life. They often can dovetail together more than you ever realize.

Financially, your world is built on the decisions that you make throughout your life. Always know the direction you want to go before you start your journey. When you make decisions without direction, your life will be like a boat without a rudder. It goes all over but doesn't actually get anywhere. The waves take the boat in multiple directions without a clear destination.

I want you to define your path and then work in harmony with that by making choices to complement it. Even with a defined path, it can be easy to make decisions that run contrary to your goals, as I discussed earlier in this chapter. When I work with individuals, I help them to not only define their path, but also to determine the types of goals that align with their paths. Then, I can help them to find the right investments and set financial goals to help them go further on that path.

Growth happens by learning from those people who inspire you to do and be more. We all have time to learn and grow.

Please email Ursula Garrett at ugarrett@cpagarrett.com or visit her website www.cpagarrett.com

Investment Success and Successful Beliefs

JASON G. CHAN

"**W**hy are you chuckling to yourself?" my brother asked as we passed by an upscale restaurant one night. "Did I miss something?"

"No, not really," I replied. "Remember those two Ferraris that were waiting for valet parking back by the restaurant that almost everybody who passed by, including us, were looking at and admiring? I just realized that if I wanted to, I could buy both of those Ferraris with cash, one for you and one for me."

Of course, I never did that. But that moment stuck in my head because it was the first time I realized that, financially, I had done okay for myself. I made my first million dollars investing in the stock market when I was just shy of 30 years old. My second million came shortly after that. That's when I stopped counting. I stopped counting because I finally found some comfort in knowing that my family was doing okay and that I was doing okay.

A few years before that, my father had suddenly passed away. It happened in 2008 in the middle of one of the greatest recessions in history. My family was entrenched in debt and my parents hardly had any retirement savings, let alone other investments. My two younger brothers and I were burdened knee-deep in student loan debt. I was living in my parents' living room because the basement where I had been living got flooded and became too moldy to stay in.

For most of my adolescent and early adult life, our family cash flow was tight, and we couldn't even afford a decent study desk. I haven't done too shabby for a boy whose desk was actually nothing more than a door flipped sideways and propped up by four poles on each corner; definitely not too shabby as an investor for someone whose degree was in fine arts and graphic design. I don't have a degree in business, finance or economics. I don't believe we need fancy degrees or education to do well in finance and investments or in life. For those who likes degrees, later in life I was told that I actually got a PhD earlier in life, since I was Poor, Hungry and Driven. At the end of the day, it's not your degrees or titles that make you, it's really about your vision and your beliefs.

YOUR BELIEFS ARE IMPORTANT

Sometimes people ask me what I did or what I invested in, hoping to get some insight as to how they too can achieve what I have. They're usually asking about specific things I did, specific things I invested in, or tools I used. What they don't understand is that these things are not the important part. Belief is where it all starts. To achieve investment success by having the proper successful beliefs, mental concepts, and proper mindset is the key.

After all, we all act and behave in certain ways because of our beliefs. Some beliefs serve us, some limit or deter us, and some set us astray. They shape what we do and how we do it. Before anything even starts, our beliefs tell us what we can do because they shape what we think is possible and what is not. Therefore, having the proper beliefs, or shaping what you already have, is really important in life, and also in investments. My purpose and goal is to help you adopt proper, empowering beliefs and realign, even discard, the negative ones as they relate to investments. It is only with a proper mindset and a successful beliefs system that you can get ahead in finances and achieve sustainable, consistent and long term investment success.

The first and, perhaps, the most important belief I want to share with you is it's possible for you to achieve financial and investment success. Not only can you achieve it, but you can achieve it on your own by empowering yourself to take control of your finances and investments. If a poor boy who started off living in a basement with a door as a study desk, who studied fine arts and graphic design, and who had large student loans and family debt could do it, so could you.

"It's Possible" is one of my favorite phrases from Les Brown. He goes on to describe that one of the keys to changing our belief system and enabling us to act on our dreams is knowing that something is possible. To know that a goal or that dream or that something we want or achieve has already been done or achieved by someone else, is to know that something is possible and achievable. More importantly, that "It's Possible" for you to achieve it too!

UNDERSTANDING FINANCE AND INVESTMENTS IS A LIFE SKILL

One of the first questions people come across when it comes to their finances and investments is, "Should I manage them myself or should I get someone else in the financial industry, such as an investment firm or bank, to manage them for me?"

Not only am I an individual investor who manages my own finances, I have also worked in the financial services industry, for one of the largest financial institutions in the country, as an investment sales representative for over 10 years. I am also a certified life coach who specializes in finance and investments. Through my various experiences, my short answer is that you should eventually invest in yourself and invest for yourself. Being able to take control and take charge of your finances and investments is a very liberating feeling that everyone should enjoy.

The investment service industry has a purpose and a place in everybody's life, but by no means should it be used or regarded as a long-term solution. It's like riding a bicycle with training wheels. Many people dream of financial freedom, but they are often dependent on an investment company to get them there. How could you be free and dependent at the same time?

Understanding finance and investments is a necessity in life. Just like eating and cooking, it's something we have to do for the rest of our lives. For this reason, I believe it's a life skill we should all acquire and develop. We have to deal with money, so we need to understand finance. Unless we spend every dime we earn or put everything under a mattress, we all have to invest. At the end of the day, nobody cares more about your financial future and well-being more than you.

HAVING SOMEONE ELSE MANAGE YOUR MONEY IS MORE COSTLY THAN YOU THINK

When it comes to eating, we won't eat out every meal, every day for the rest of our lives. We won't do that because we know it doesn't make sense and it gets expensive. So why would it make sense to pay someone else or a company to manage your investments every day for the rest of your life? Well, many people actually do that. One of the main reasons is because the investment industry has presented their fees in a way that seems deceivingly small and inexpensive. That's why many people don't mind "dining out" their whole lives.

Let's use the mutual fund industry as an example. The mutual fund industry is what most people are exposed to and familiar with when it comes to professional investment management. Aside from possible front-load and back-load fees and commissions, all mutual funds charge what they call a management expense ratio or MER. The MER alone for the average mutual fund ranges from approximately 2% - 2.5% a year. We'll take the low end of 2% to give them the benefit of the doubt. A 2% annual fee sounds small and nominal, doesn't it? The financial industry usually does not take the time or effort to explain what this fee actually means. Often customers are left with the impression that they get charged 2% MER from the gains that the company makes for them, if any.

In reality, that 2% MER is calculated and charged based on the entire amount of money they are managing for the customer, or what they call assets under management. What that means is, if you give them $100 to invest, they will charge you 2% on that $100, so essentially $2. Say you have $100,000 invested with them. At 2% MER, that works out to be $2,000 a year. For those who wish to have $1,000,000 ($1 Million dollars) a 2% MER would cost them $20,000 a year! To look at it from another perspective, a 2% MER fee in 5 years alone, works out to 10% (2% x 5). In 10 years, that works out to be 20% (2% x 10). In a mere 5 years and 10 years respectively, you would have paid out 10% and 20% of your hard-earned money in MER fees. Now consider that most people save and invest for retirement for about 35 years, how does the math work out for a long duration like that?

As I mentioned, the financial and investment industry is a business. Just like the restaurant industry and eating out, there is a time and place for services like that. However, it should not be used as a long-term solution, because it becomes very costly in the long run. I feel a true investment company and professional should be promoting financial freedom and independence, not financial dependence. Understanding finance and investments is truly a life skill that we should all acquire and develop. We can't afford not to.

In the examples above, I purposely kept the math simple and to the point and avoided financial jargon, such as compounding, time value, etc., because those are the kind of things that deter from the basic idea and confuse clients. The investment industry will critique our example and try to say that they will grow the client's money through the years. However, at the end of day, they cannot guarantee you any gains. So we won't factor that in. And to be fair, I won't assume they'll lose your money either. I kept it neutral in my example— no gains, no losses—similar to the "lost decade" that we experienced in the stock markets not too long ago.

INVESTING IS LIKE TREASURE HUNTING

When most people think of the world of investments and finance it seems overwhelmingly complex. A simple and interesting analogy I use to compare the world of investing and the investment industry is a big treasure hunt. If we were to look at it from this perspective, we would get a better understanding of how things work, many things would become apparent and begin to make sense.

So off to treasure hunting we go. Imagine we are in a world where treasure hunting is a big deal and almost everybody is out to find some treasure. Opinions on how to find treasure are a dime a dozen and everybody has their ideas and opinions.

Yet, despite the abundance of ideas and strategies floating around, many of these ideas tend to be passed around by people who have never found any significant treasure themselves. They hear and get these ideas and concepts from family members, a friend, a friend of a friend, and various media outlets. And where did many of these ideas originate from? A lot of these ideas actually came about through the "treasure hunting industry."

Yes, treasure hunting is such a big deal, there's actually a treasure hunting industry which is supposedly there to help you and guide you to find treasure. There are big corporate institutions with many employees who sell you treasure maps, treasure guides, strategies, tools and gadgets along with various products and services which they claim will help you find treasure. Many of them offer packaged plans to help treasure hunt for you through their professional and experienced treasure hunters.

The deal is that you put up all the capital to be used for the treasure hunt, but they do not guarantee you any success. The only guarantee is that they will charge you a management fee whether or not they find you treasure. And if they do end up finding treasure, they actually take a bigger cut of your money. So you put up all the money and take all the risk and they take a risk free payment from you in order to help you treasure hunt. And there are no guarantees of success. It's a pretty good business model for them, but not such a good business idea for you.

At some point you might begin to wonder that if these companies and their staff are so good at treasure hunting, how come they just don't focus on that and treasure hunt for themselves? Eventually, you'll realize that these companies actually make money from selling treasure hunting packages and products and by providing treasure hunting services. They don't make their money from actually finding treasure, per se.

Their frontline staff, sales representatives and professional treasure hunters, can give you all sorts of treasure hunting advice, ideas, and strategies, along with various treasure products and services the company has to offer. However, like most regular people, most of them have never found success in treasure hunting. The majority of their income actually comes from working their sales jobs and earning commission selling treasure hunting packages, products and services.

Sometimes you see some of these sales people enjoying the luxuries of life which can create the impression that they have actually found treasure from treasure hunting, but the reality is, they were actually just a successful sales person, not a successful treasure hunter.

Remember how we said that much of the common investment advice that floats around in public originated from these treasure hunting companies in the treasure hunting industry? A lot of the time this supposed treasure hunting advice is actually based on half-truths that are either outdated, have lost effectiveness, or have never been useful at all. They are mainly ideas and strategies used to promote and sell various treasure hunting packages, products and services.

There are actually really good and skillful treasure hunters out there. As you would expect, most of them spend their time treasure hunting for themselves. Some do open up treasure hunting companies to help others find treasure, but they usually require clients with lots of money and many of them have reached capacity and have stopped taking on new clients.

Keep this treasure hunting analogy in mind the next time you think about investments and the investment industry. It should give you an idea of how to make sense of it all and help you decide if you really wish to have someone else treasure hunt for you or not.

THE INVESTMENT LANDSCAPE HAS CHANGED

Since the new millennium, the stock market and investment landscape has been a lot different than it was in previous decades. This is not just a belief—it is a fact. It is important that we recognize and acknowledge this reality and incorporate it into our belief system for two main reasons.

First of all, in order to invest successfully and navigate through the stock market, we need to understand what kind of landscape and environment we are currently in. Imagine you are taking a road trip, how could you expect a to get from point A to point B if you were using an old and dated road map from many decades ago? I am sure it would be a frustrating trip with a few wrong turns here and there.

Secondly, understanding how the stock market and investment landscape used to be can help us understand where many investment ideas and strategies we still hear and read about came to be. More important is why they have lost relevance, effectiveness and significance.

Using the beginning of the new millennium, the year 2000, as a benchmark for the midpoint year of reference, let us take a look at the last 36 years of the S&P500, a popular and widely followed North American stock index. We will take a look and compare the 18 years prior to the new millennium and 18 years since the new millennium. So from 1982 to 2000, compared to 2000 to 2018.

In terms of returns, if you were to just buy and hold from the beginning of 1982 to the beginning of 2000, the 18 years prior to 2000, the total return of the S&P 500 was approximately 1,100%. From the beginning of 2000 to the beginning of 2018, the last 18 years, the total return of the S&P 500 was approximately 92%. A 1,110% return compared to a 92% return. That's a difference of almost 12 times.

In terms of declines and recovery, between 1982 and 2000, the two biggest drops were Black Monday of 1987, which saw an approximately 36% drop from top to bottom, which took 8 months to break even, and August of 1998 which saw an approximately 23% drop from top to bottom, which took less than 2 months to break even.

In terms of declines and recovery, between 2000 and 2018, the two biggest drops were an approximately 50% drop during the years from early 2000 to early 2003. If you happened to have bought at the peak, it would have taken you about 7.5 years to break even. Then an approximately 57% drop from mid 2007 to early 2009. If you happened to have bought at the peak, it would have taken you about 6 years to break even.

From 1982 to 2000, there was a 23% to 36% drop, with a recovery time of 2 to 8 months, compared to the years from 2000 to 2018, in which there was a 50% to 57% drop, with a recovery time of 6 to 7.5 years. From declines to recoveries, there was a dramatic difference in magnitude.

To summarize, it is important that we recognize and acknowledge that the investment landscape has changed a lot in the last 20 years because many investment strategies and ideologies we still hear today were developed during that comparatively stable and less volatile time. However, due to the changes we have seen in the last 20 years, many of these strategies and ideologies have lost their effectiveness, value, and relevance. The conclusion is, since our investment landscape has changed and evolved, we too need to evolve and adapt our investment strategies to the present. We cannot just keep on blindly using what has worked in the past.

WE INVEST IN OUR BELIEFS, NOT THE MARKETS

As we started off by mentioning, beliefs are very important when it comes to investing. They affect how we invest: if we take charge of our investments ourselves, have someone else invest for us or if we even invest at all. More importantly, I have to stress the importance of adopting the right and proper beliefs because ultimately when we are investing, we are investing in our beliefs. People often think they are investing in the markets, but actually what they are investing in is their beliefs about the markets. This is a critical concept to keep in mind. Personally, understanding and realizing that concept helped take my investments to the next level.

This reality might be a little difficult to wrap our heads around at first, but consider this, the markets behave the same for everyone. If we are just investing in the markets, we should all get similar if not identical results. But we don't. How come some people make more money than others in a rising market, for example? Or how come some are able to profit from a recession while others lose a fortune? The market's behaviour and performance does not vary from one person to another. It is the beliefs about the markets that vary from one person to another. Therefore, one of the main keys to being able to invest successfully is to have the proper beliefs in regards to investing and the markets.

GENUINE INVESTMENT ADVICE AND POOR INVESTMENT ADVICE

Many of our beliefs regarding investments have been acquired and shaped by various pieces of investment advice we've come across over time. And there's all sorts of investment concepts, strategies, and theories. Which ones serves us? Which ones do not? There was a time when it was tough getting information, let alone getting information in a timely manner. But today, with the evolution of technology via computers, smartphones and the internet, we live in a time of information overload. Investment ideas and strategies are a dime a dozen. Almost everyone seems to have an idea of what to do. We come across so many investment ideas and so much advice. Often, the more we learn the more confused we get, as many of these investment ideas seem to contradict each other. How do we organize and conceptualize them all in a context that makes sense? As an individual investor I, too, had to struggle with that problem.

After years of study, research and practical hands-on experience investing my own money, as well as working in the finance and investment sales industry, I was finally able to sort and put everything in context. This belief system is a mental construct meant to organize all the ideas, advice, theories, strategies, and concepts I've accumulated as they relate to investments. I'll just refer to all of that as "investment advice" for simplicity.

It's obvious there's some investment advice that works and some that does not. So, I separate them into two categories: "Genuine Investment Advice" and "Poor Investment Advice." Within those two categories, there are actually two sub-categories we could further separate the investment advice into.

Within Genuine Investment Advice, the first subcategory is investment advice that I believe is almost universal and works for almost everyone. For example, diversification, cutting losses short, letting winners grow, and waiting for favourable risk to return opportunities before investing.

The second subcategory, as well as all the other categories we'll touch upon, is where things get interesting. It's where it causes lots of confusion among people's belief systems and is a source of frustration for many. Within this second sub-category of Genuine Investment Advice is the investment advice that is accurate and works but may not work for everyone, because it depends on their personality and their investment style. For example, many investment ideas, theories, and strategies seem like complete opposites when you compare them with one another: value investing versus momentum investing, swing trading versus momentum investing, fundamental analysis versus technical analysis, short-term trading versus long-term investing, buy low and sell high versus buy high and sell higher, and top down versus bottom up investment styles. All these investment ideas and strategies work, but success depends on how they match the individual investor's personality and how they are used alongside their investment style. In a nutshell, those are examples of Genuine Investment Advice.

On the other end of the spectrum from Genuine Investment Advice we have Poor Investment Advice. It's basically advice that is not effective or does not work. Within this main category, it also has two sub-categories.

In the first sub-category is investment advice that used to work but is outdated because of the change in the investment landscape that we touched upon earlier. It used to work and perhaps even used to deliver great results but has since greatly lost value and effectiveness. Yet, these investment ideas still get passed around by many people because they have failed to recognize that the investment landscape has dramatically changed and evolved in recent years.

Some examples are: index investing, buying and holding indiscriminately, dollar cost averaging, and investing on a consistent and regular schedule regardless of overall market conditions. It's easy to see where such investment ideas, strategies and advice come from once we understand how the investment landscape used to be and what had happened in the past. Like we've seen in our example, the stock market, namely the S&P500, went up approximately 1,100% from 1982 to the year 2000. Yet, in our recent investment landscape from 2000 to the beginning of 2018, the total return of the S&P500 was a mere 92%—a return that's dramatically less than 1/12th in the same 18-year time span. That is less than 10% of the 1,100% return the we've seen from 1982 to the year 2000.

The second subcategory of Poor Investment Advice is the one which I despise the most. They are essentially "investment advice" that was never effective and never worked. For example, advice such as "If you don't sell your losing position, you aren't really losing money because unless you cash out, it's only a paper loss." That is as foolish as saying "If you go to the casino and convert your cash into casino chips, then you lose your chips, you're not actually losing money unless you convert those chips back into cash." Then there's "Adding to losses and losing positions is beneficial because when you average down, it gives you better value and a lower overall price point." With this strategy, you are not only not cutting your losses, you are adding to an already losing position. Technically, you could use this flawed logic to invest in a company as it goes all the way down to bankruptcy because it suggests the lower the price goes, the more you should invest. There is also "Focus on the long-term, and don't worry that your stocks are down because you're still getting paid dividends." Focusing solely on dividends presents a very distorted and partial picture, as you should be focusing on total return which consists of dividends plus any capital gains or losses. With that in mind, if your stock is down -40%, it would be foolish to say it's alright because you're receiving a 3% dividend yield.

People often ask, "If such investment advice doesn't work, then why do people say these things?" The answer is because these ideas mainly originate and get spread around by unscrupulous individuals in the financial and investment industry. In reality, such investment advice was merely conjured up to promote and sell investment products to customers and keep their customers invested so they could continue to charge them various fees and commissions.

Unfortunately, because much of this investment advice came from individuals within the financial and investment industry, it gave them a false sense of credibility and such bad advice got perpetually circulated. This is especially true because the advice is usually mixed in with some rationalization and half truths. When I say half truths, I am also referring to the dated investment advice that we mentioned earlier. I consider those half truths, because those strategies used to work, but have greatly lost significance since. Nevertheless, such bad advice is still often used as sales pitches by individuals in the industry to promote and sell various investment products.

Notice that all such advice falls under a similar underlying idea. It is to tell the customer that it is always a good time to invest and once they are invested, to never sell. For example, when the markets are high, they will say you should invest more because things are going well and you are making money. When the markets are low, they will say you should invest more because you are getting good value. Also, it is always a good time to invest, regardless of how the overall market condition is, because it is supposedly about your time in the markets, not timing the markets. Basically, the message is always geared at giving them your money, keeping it with them and never taking it away, so they can continuously charge you various fees. At the end of the day, if the client makes money, all the better, but even if they don't, the individual and company still gets to charge their fees.

In providing Genuine Investment Advice verses Poor Investment Advice, an individual's salary and bonus often comes in between the two. I'm reminded of a quote from Upton Sinclair: "It is difficult to get a man to understand something, when his salary depends on his not understanding it." However, to be fair, many of those who work in the financial and investment industry are not unscrupulous or ill-intentioned. Like many everyday people, they too, are caught up in the confusion. They come across poor investment advice that they actually believe to be true, which they use themselves and also end up passing on.

ADDITIONAL INVESTMENT TIPS FOR THE EVERYDAY INVESTOR

Make Use of Technical Analysis

As individual investors, we have limited time and resources. I believe the most efficient and effective way for an individual investor to conduct market research and to look for investment opportunities is through the use of technical analysis. Before you get intimidated, technical analysis is basically a fancy way of saying to look at price charts and graphs. You are literally looking at a picture, the big picture. It's efficient because, for example, if I wanted to, I could literally look through hundreds of companies and their price charts in a day. Comparatively, I cannot read through hundreds of annual reports or articles a day.

Keep an Investing Journal

Experiencing losses due to bad judgements or mistakes is part of every investor's journey. Unfortunately, when it comes to investing, making mistakes usually translates to losing money. At least when losses and mistakes occur, try to profit from them by keeping a journal of what happened and how, in an effort to learn from the experience and to not to let it happen again. As the saying goes, "Fool me once, shame on you. Fool me twice, shame on me."

Be Sure to Diversify

Diversification is a simple risk management technique we should all make use of to protect ourselves from the unknown and to improve our risk to return ratio. The simple reason being we can never foresee and predict everything in the markets. During my years of investing, I've seen an oil company whose oil rig was destroyed by a natural disaster; a factory that, due to some employee's negligence, was burned down to a crisp; the CEO of a company who got caught up in various alleged scandals leading to the collapse of the company and, one of my favorites, which is when Tesla's stock price took a sudden dive one day because Elon Musk decided to announce that the company was going bankrupt as an April Fool's Day joke in 2018. No matter how much in-depth research we conduct, nobody could have foreseen any of those events happening. So protect your investment portfolio by diversifying.

Look Beyond "Glam Stocks"

When individuals share their investment holdings with me, I often notice that they have many of the same stock holdings. The reason is they often have what I call "Glam Stocks." These are the glamorous stocks we often hear about in the news and media, the ones our friends and family talk about at dinner parties and gatherings. There is nothing wrong with having those holdings per se, but expand your scope, look further and dig deeper. You will realize that there are plenty of more diverse opportunities out there, many of which are either less volatile and less risky, have more growth potential, have a better performance record or sometimes all of the above. So keep looking and don't settle just for what you hear or see around you.

Know When to Get Out, Before You Get In

Before you get into an investment position, decide when you would exit if things do not go as intended. You are more clear minded before you start an investment. So decide when you would exit if things do not go your way ahead of time, as you will lose objectivity afterwards.

Gradually Ease In and Out of Investments

When investing, especially in stocks, a common practice is to use one entry and one exit into an investment position. Instead of using an all-in or all-out approach, a more strategic risk management approach would be to gradually ease yourself in and out of an investment depending on its subsequent performance. For example, instead of investing $5,000 all at once, consider investing initially only $2,500, then decide if you still want to invest the remaining $2,500 depending on the subsequent performance of the particular investment. Doing this would automatically cut your initial risk by 50%. The same idea applies to getting out of an investment.

Cut Losses and Keep Them Small

When investing, keeping control of our losses is a vital component of risk management. If there is one common piece of advice I've gathered from many great investors, it is that they all cut their losses and keep them small. Considering that most big losses usually started off as small losses, there is no point in letting a small loss grow into a big loss. If you are uncertain about an investment holding, instead of holding all of it or none of it, consider selling a portion of it. For example, if you sell half of it, you will reduce your risk by 50%. Another common culprit that leads investors to hold onto losses is focusing on break-even points and prices. In reality, nobody actually cares where or at what price you bought an investment and where you would break-even. It has no special meaning to anybody other than you and the tax department, so do not focus on that.

Avoid Adding to Losing Positions

When you have a losing investment position, often people believe that buying more will get you better value as you average down your overall price point. That is actually a poor strategy because having a losing position usually means that something you anticipated did not materialize and instead the opposite outcome occurred. There must have been something that was misjudged, overlooked, or unforeseen. Therefore, it does not make strategic sense to add more to an investment which you have already misunderstood and misjudged. Moreover, not only does that go against the concept of keeping your losses small, it is in fact the opposite, because you are adding more money to a losing position.

Remember that You Are Investing in Your Beliefs, Not the Markets

If there is one piece of advice that is more important than controlling your losses, it would definitely be that nobody cares more about your financial well-being than you. So understanding finance and investments is a life skill you should not only acquire but develop, and it all starts with your beliefs. At the core of it all, it is about working on developing your investment belief system.

This requires realigning and readjusting your beliefs and perhaps adopting new ones that serve you, while discarding those that do not. Remember that at the end of the day, we are all just investing in our beliefs.

FINAL THOUGHTS

Finance and investments are one of my greatest passions. I hope I was able to share some fresh perspectives and unique insights on subjects that I personally find to be rarely touched upon or discussed. The ideas and concepts are not exhaustive or complete, however, these are the big ideas, essential concepts and quintessential core beliefs that I've acquired through the years and which really helped propel my investment understanding and financial success.

Often there is nothing worse than to listen to someone advising you on how to reach your goals, when they have not actually reached it themselves. If there was a way for me to turn back time and have the opportunity to sit down with some successful investors who were willing to give me a few important pointers about finance and investing over a cup of coffee or a meal, I hope they would have shared with me the same pointers and beliefs I have shared with you in the last few pages. I know the insights would have definitely made my investment and financial experience a lot smoother and would have helped me reach my financial goals a lot sooner. These beliefs I'm talking about have helped me through many hurdles, make many investment breakthroughs and achieve financial success. I hope they will do the same for you. Remember, "It's Possible!"

For more investment insight, techniques and strategies, visit:
InvestingItWisely.com

Your Life Energy

AMAL INDI

I have 20 years of experience in the tech sector and corporate banking. In my previous life in the "Rat Race", I was waking up every day and going to a job that provided well for me. After some major changes in my life (including a divorce), I started recognizing that I wasn't intrinsically happy. I would be going about my day filled with negative thoughts and emotions. It felt as though they were taking over in a way, and I recognized how they were beginning to affect every moment of my day and every interaction with those around me. I refer to these as "Thought Bugs", which I will go on to explain later. These Thought Bugs were almost like a computer virus, affecting all the thoughts or, as one may say, programming in my mind. After recognizing these Bugs and studying them in myself for many years, I began to draw strong conclusions about how I could create positive change in my mind. This positive change in my thoughts would eventually lead to me leaving the "Rat Race" and starting on the mission of my life to share my new paradigm with those around me. I believe that we can change our minds and create a positive and uplifting life, not only for ourselves, but for those around us. I would love to share with you the basics of what I discovered, a new way of examining our thought patterns and how to drastically shift the energy around you (your Aura) so that you can lead a fantastic life!

GETTING STARTED ON YOUR OWN JOURNEY

When was the last time you really felt 100%? When I say 100%, I mean you wake up feeling a general positivity in your mood, you are looking forward to a new day, your interactions with people feel good, and you walk around feeling a general sense of purpose even with the simple tasks of getting groceries or whatever your work environment. You may think that you have no say in how you really feel. That deep down, you cannot control your thoughts and emotions. I know that this is not true. I developed a unique way of seeing our minds and how deeply they affect our energy. Have you heard of life energy, such as positive energy, negative energy, Aura energy, and universal energy? Read on!

WHAT MAKES US HUMAN?

Each one of us is a biological marvel of different cells, tissues, genes. These are the many working pieces that come together to create our human body. What really makes us human in a whole sense? We each possess an in-depth energetic landscape that we can't deny. This energetic pulse is used by scientists and technicians daily to perform tests and create pictures of our bodies and their functions. Think of the neuroscientists that connect our bodies to electrodes and measure our brain waves. That's part of it. We can't deny there is a part of us beyond just the tissues of our muscles and bones.

Did you know that surrounding you right now is an energy field that is all your own? This energetic field is referred to as your Aura. This Aura can be the beginning of a life that you love. Every human being has an energy field around them. We cannot see this field with the naked eye. However, we can see this field with an Aura machine. It's true! I personally have had mine captured and what was reflected back to me (in terms of energetic levels) was what I was truly feeling.

Your Aura and the energy you radiate is 100% in your control. Some days, you might feel positive and good, while other days, you may feel more negative and lower. These are your energy levels. They can vibrate high or low. It depends on you and your thoughts. Remember, with improvements to your mind and thoughts, your aura energy field will continuously change, thus altering the life you are leading.

YOUR AURA

Over the centuries of humans existing and contemplating our existence, many have acknowledged the fact that we have an energy that extends beyond our skin and flesh, which can actually interact with the world around us. This is referred to as your body's Aura. The Aura refers to the energy around your body that can be affected from the inside out or the outside in. When it is strong, the Aura around your body can extend quite a way beyond the barrier of your physical body (your skin). It can also manifest as different colours, depending on the emotional mood of the person. For example, when you are in a state of calm, then you will exude a white Aura. When you are in a state of anger, then you will exude a red Aura. Sometimes Auras may also be a combination of different colours. There is technology now that can show the colour and strength of someone's Aura. I have had mine checked. One day, it was light in colour and extended far beyond my body. This didn't surprise me as I feel I live in a state of calm, clear energy and my inner emotional landscape is positive. If you were to have an opportunity to get yours checked today what do you think the results would be? Strong and white? Or weak and maybe red? Maybe you feel like it may not show up at all.

This is what I want to teach you. This is my mission right now: To help you understand that you can empower yourself and create a strong, positive Aura that will not only affect your overall sense of well-being. It will affect your relationships, your business, and your life as a whole.

YOUR HUMAN SYSTEM

Through my own exploration, I began seeing and noticing a pattern in how my Aura was being affected by different things in my life. As I continued to study this in myself, it became clear to me that that there were specific things in play, and it was all rooted in my mind. Having a strong background in technology, I began to clearly see how our own minds behave like supercomputers. (Stay with me here!) Just like a super computer, we have our own operating system and the ability to run many programs at once. We are constantly juggling responsibilities, taking in the world around us, assessing how we feel, and determining what we need. The list could go on and on! Just take a moment right now: close your eyes and connect to all the "programs" open in your mind that are constantly running. Relate that to being connected to your own unique operating system of your mind. Now imagine that a computer virus was implanted into one of your programs and began affecting your thoughts. Computer viruses are designed to spread to all parts of a computer with the goal of eventually changing the computer, more often than not, making it completely dysfunctional. This is what can happen in your mind. A negative thought may enter your mind about something specific. Maybe a co-worker engages you in conversation about a rumour that someone is up for raise (one that you applied for) or on your coffee break the barista makes a mistake on your order and you feel it ruins your morning. I call these viruses of our thoughts Human Errors. In its most basic form, Human Errors can be outlined as the following emotions, or what I like to call Thought Bugs:

- Anger
- Suspicion
- Craving
- Comparison
- Low self-esteem
- Procrastination
- Getting stuck in negative thoughts

What it can be boiled down to is that these negative thought bugs can enter into your mind, which in turn creates negative energy. This leads to stress and a weakening of your Aura.

I'm sure you can think of a definitive moment, probably even within the last day or the last week, where you can see how your own errors were affecting your core system and negatively impacting the energy around you.

Luckily, we have a set of more positive emotions and various ways of reacting that counter the negative ones. I have identified these and aptly named them our Human Features.

Primary Human features that combat the errors include:

- Love and kindness
- Acceptance
- Forgiveness
- Courageousness
- Patience
- Authenticity
- Gratefulness

One can think of these features as a built-in tool box to combat negativity. This is always at our disposal! I want to help you identify where these positive emotions are in you, so that you may have access them and strengthen the energy that you are putting out into the world and your Aura.

Look, I am not a psychologist. I am not a therapist. I am, however, a believer in how we show up to our work and interact with those around us will have a deep impact on the life we are creating for ourselves. I have firsthand experience. I have taken myself from a place of negativity and darkness to a place of possibility. I have watched my newfound passions and work flourish, along with my relationships, personal and otherwise.

This is a different way of looking at things. This just isn't your usual "Be positive" message. This is connecting into the fact that as humans, we have a distinct design in place to help us truly create a good life for ourselves. The foundation of this is to truly feel happy and positive from the inside out, so that what we engage with is affected by our positive energy. Think of the last time you had an encounter with someone who you felt emitted a positive or happy energy? How did it make you feel? How did you react? You truly have the power to combat these negative thought processes (bugs) already in you! Don't you want to be the one truly living in your potential and sharing your positivity with everyone and everything in your life?

THE "AWESOME LIFE" IS WAITING FOR YOU!

Let's get down to business. Thanks for sticking with me. If you have continued reading to this point, then I want to applaud you! It means that you are deeply interested in living your best life.

Side effects of a mind free from negative Thought Bugs may include:
- General feelings of happiness and relaxation
- Genuine connections when meeting people
- A mind free from clutter
- A deep appreciation for the world and people around you
- High levels of productivity
- Willingness to learn new skills
- Gaining more contacts and connections with ease
- Feeling an authentic excitement for projects and self-development
- Being ready to rock your life!

These are just a few of the feelings available to you if you commit to removing negative Thought Bugs from your life, thus strengthening your energy and Aura from the inside out. I wouldn't be here today if I didn't do the work and experience the benefits of being on the other side of the process.

BRING LIGHT TO YOU

My hope for you is to learn how to identify your negative Thought Bugs and stop their process of multiplication. For you to empower yourself with positivity and strengthen your aura. For you to leave feelings of depletion behind and bring your energy back to 100%. For you to share your positive energy with the world and make it a better place!

Never forget: An Awesome Life is within your reach at all times. I believe it. In fact, I will go so far as to say I know it is. I have taken my own life and made it awesome by taking all I have outlined in my work and applying it to myself. Now it is your turn to turn up the positivity in your life and let your Aura shine!

I encourage you to check out my website, www.happinessmountain.com, to receive a free guide on removing your negative energy. In this guide, you will also be given a sneak peek into the app I am developing. The Happiness Mountain™ app will quickly become your new best friend! I developed the Happiness Mountain™ app to be a way to actually track those negative Thought Bugs and coach you to clear your worries and boost your energy levels! By giving you this important tool at your fingertips, I know you will be able to strengthen your energy and basically start living a more happy life! If you haven't guessed already, I love technology and its possibilities for enhancing our lives. I can't wait for you to be one of the first people to try this app and reap its benefits right away at www.happinessmountain.com/app.

BRINGING LIGHT TO YOU SO THAT YOU MAY BRING LIGHT TO THE WORLD

Now that I have given you some insight on how you can truly change your life by changing your own energy, I want to share the ways that Happiness Mountain™ can help you begin to apply these concepts. The process of understanding, application, and execution is key when committing to changing the way your mind functions and, over time, changing your aura.

Now that you know you have the power to change your life via your thoughts, I wonder why you wouldn't want to act now to change your life. Your own personal idea of an awesome life is within reach! I left behind an old way of living and being in order to start on a new path. I am confident that you have the power to do that for yourself as well. We all just need a little help. To be honest, I wish I had connected with these deeper levels of understanding regarding my thoughts and how they affect my life earlier. However, as we all know, timing is everything, especially when it comes to your advancement on both a personal level and a business one. Take this as a sign that it may be time for you to dive into these deep changes. The techniques, once you really begin to understand them, are quite straightforward. I know that you live a busy life and are striving to do your best. However, it takes commitment to change. Why not start now?

Happiness Mountain™ can offer you many tools to get started and help you dive deeper. The first step is easy! I encourage you to head over to my website www.happinessmountain.com to sign up and stay connected to the developments in my work. You will automatically receive an easy to follow guide on how to remove your negative energy, which will be delivered right to your inbox! You will also be given an automatic sneak peek into my app.

THE HAPPINESS MOUNTAIN™ APP

I am constantly inspired by how we connect online through different platforms and technologies. I believe that this can be the start to a great change in how we grow and develop. I designed the app as a convenient way for you to connect to your energy boosting practices on the go. We all spend some time on our phones scrolling and engaging on different platforms. Why not invest that time mindfully instead of mindlessly? The Happiness Mountain™ app, www.happinessmountain.com/app, helps you do that by having the tools you can utilize to boost your own positive energy available at any time!

Features include the following:

- Troubleshooting what is worrying you and replacing that worry with positivity

- Ways to resolve disputes without creating negative energy and affecting your Aura

- Aura boosting activities you can do on daily basis, while tracking your progress with your own private point system

- An emergency toolkit for handling sudden negative situations

- An easy guide to all the Thought Bugs and how to handle them available at a touch of your screen, so that you may continue to learn how you can change your thoughts to more positive ones and keep your positive energy high!

HAPPINESS MOUNTAIN™ FOR KIDS

Calling all parents and anyone who takes care of children! This work isn't just applicable to more mature minds and bodies. It can start when we are young! I am in the process of finishing development on a series of books for children that will cover all the core concepts of my work and Happiness Mountain™, so that we may share these valuable tools and concepts even with the developing minds of the next generation. Of course, there will be interactive games for children as well, because as we all know that some of the best learning happens when we are having fun! This goes for adults too, don't you think? Stay in the loop by connecting with me at www.happinessmountain.com.

MY NEXT BOOK

I am ready to dive deeper and share with you even more in my new book, *Happiness Mountain™: Double Your Happiness, Awesomeness and Spirituality*. In the book we are going to explore deeper than ever before. *Happiness Mountain™* will go more in depth on how you can harness the three levels of energy (Positive/Negative, Aura and Universal) to change your perspective and unlock your perfect life. I want to share with you the techniques and deep processes that will affect all aspects of your life. Remember those 'Negative Thought Bugs' I was talking about earlier? In my new book I will teach you not only how to eliminate them, I want to teach you how to protect yourself from future encounters with 'Negative Thought Bugs' therefore truly creating change in your life for the better. You will also learn techniques on how to recharge your energy, boost your aura and use your new skills for resolving conflicts and affecting your business.

I want you to harness the power of your personal Positive & Aura energies, learn to dance with the Universal energy that is always at your disposable and be able to live at a level of existence that falls in line with your ideal, perfect life. Take a look at the *Happiness Mountain™* diagram on the next page. You can define your perfect life as living with a high level of inner peace, the level of inner happiness. Your Awesome Life and Spiritual Life revolves around being of service to others and helping others. You can live a combination of all levels of the *Happiness Mountain™*. Whatever you personally define as perfection is where you have the power.

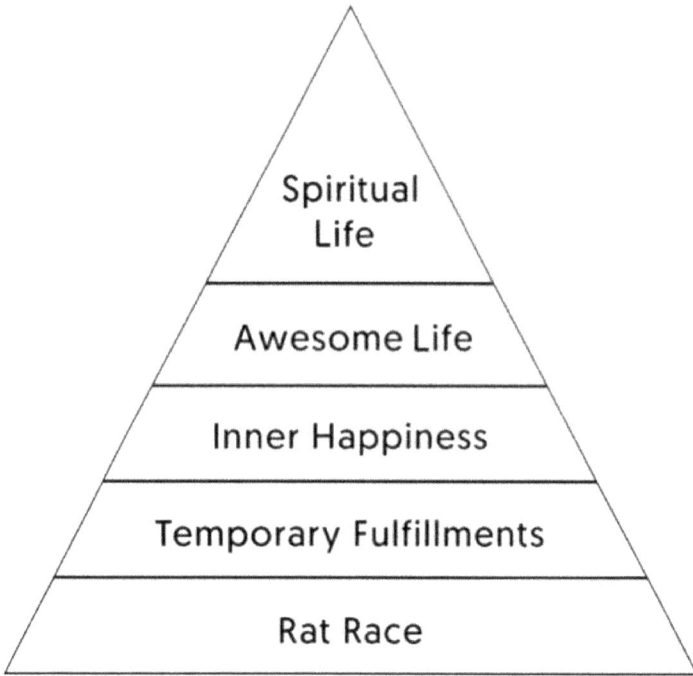

Happiness Mountain^TM created by Amal Indi

Some might argue you cannot have a perfect life. I say you already have a perfect life and it is blocked by negative energy from coming into full fruition. This negative energy can be existing as a low self-esteem bug or a comparison bug. You may define perfect life as comparing to others. You may try to achieve things with craving energy. Please remember: You are already whole, complete and perfect. You cannot access your full power because of the negative energy being generated by your thoughts. When you learn to remove those negative thoughts as I teach you in *Happiness Mountain^TM*, you will realize how much power you have in life. This will be your turning point to harness the energy to power-up your personal, business and spiritual life! In the book I will give you all the tools and techniques to accomplish that. After reading my new book *Happiness Mountain^TM* you will be able to shift your life to a new paradigm that is not only accessible but exciting. How do you think it will feel to lead a perfect life? Can you think of even one thing that may change for the better if you decided to investigate how you could crush your negative energies, enhance your positive energies and essentially eliminate future worries from your life? ... Wow! I am excited for you just thinking about it myself! I know the profound changes it created for me in my life and I look forward to hearing how it affects yours.

YOU CAN LEAD AN AWESOME LIFE

My hope for you is to learn how to identify your negative Thought Bugs and stop their process of multiplication. For you to empower yourself with positivity and strengthen your aura. For you to leave feelings of depletion behind and bring your energy back to 100%. For you to share your positive energy with the world and make it a better place!

Never forget: The Awesome Life is within your reach at all times. I believe it. In fact, I will go as so far to say I know it is. I have taken my own life and made it perfect in my eyes by taking all I have outlined in my work and applying it to myself. Again, your negative thoughts may say your life is not perfect, which might include your low self-esteem, cravings, or comparison bugs blocking you. Don't let these bugs create negative energy. Instead, clear them and power-up the personal, business, or spiritual aspects of your life. Never forget you have the power over your own mind- NOT your negative Thought Bugs. Now it is time to power-up the positivity in your life and let your Aura shine!

I encourage you to check out my website, www.happinessmountain.com, for the opportunity to stay connected to the global community of people who have already begun to use this work to boost their positivity and create their

Awesome Life in their personal, business, and spiritual domains. I can't wait for you to begin using The Happiness Mountain™ App to start training your energy to stay positive and even get stronger. Of course, I encourage you to visit www.happinessmountain.com to stay connected and be in the know as to what is coming down the pipeline with this life changing work.

I have dedicated my life to bringing these concepts and work to you. I know you can change your energy and begin to not only affect your own life, but the entire world. I believe deeply that when as many people as possible align their energy to a higher, more positive state, then we can truly make a collective difference. Let's start today!

Amal Indi lives in Vancouver, Canada, and is the founder and CEO of Happiness Mountain™ Inc. After 20 years of working in technology and corporate banking, Amal is on a mission to give people the possibility to live with their full potential in their personal, business, and spiritual domains. He has found innovative techniques and tools to remove negative energy and power up your personal life, business life, and spiritual life. Ultimately, you can make the world a more awesome place for everyone. He believes that technology has the potential to transform the minds and energy of people and facilitate change. Amal wants to help people around the globe live a positive and enriching life through the energy-based tools and techniques of this innovative system he has developed to strengthen your energy and help you live a life full of happiness and potential. Find his story and work at www.happinessmountain.com.

The Speed of Light

Live and Thrive in the Flow When It Gets Too Much Too Fast

VALERIE KANAY HART

If you want to find the secrets of the universe, think in terms of energy,
frequency and vibration.

-Nikola Tesla

LAY DOWN THE LAW

The Law of Vibration tells us that EVERYTHING vibrates in constant motion. That includes the stars overhead, the ground on which we stand and you and I! Our minds tell us that we are solid bodies with a fixed sense of self, but on an energetic level we are changing and shifting all the time. Today, many of us feel that our world is accelerating, spinning on its axis faster and faster. It can feel like too much too fast, but we have to keep the pace in order to avoid being left behind. You have to step up your game and you have to know what to do and when to do it, right? The pivotal question then becomes, with all of life speeded up, how fast do you want to change and how fast can you fully change? If you're serious about transformation, then the answer must be: at the speed of light!

Change at this speed happens effortlessly when you start living your life in the flow. Discover how to slip into the flow in my book The Speed of Light, which will help you create a new vibrant, healthy, and loving relationship with your truth. You must align our mind-body connection to the God of your own understanding, and you can only thrive when you act on every available opportunity to move your lives forward. Visit www.thespeedoflightbook. com to learn why and how your life becomes more meaningful and abundant when you have a worthwhile ambition to pursue.

SHIFTING SIGNALS

Everything is happening faster and faster, and we are the champions of personal evolution. That statement may not describe you right now because you feel stuck in a rut. Maybe you are feeling that you are standing still while the rest of the world is passing you by. If you are, I urge you to commit to breaking the shackles that keep you stuck. When you do, you will begin to experience richer, deeper connections for a more meaningful life. You will also gain the freedom to do what you love, choosing when you want to do it and how you like it to be done. You are a born winner and will succeed. Get the tools you need for success at www.thespeedoflightbook.com.

You know you are stuck when you cannot seem to create change in your life, no matter what you do. To get out of this rut requires becoming aware of the signals you are sending out into your personal vibrational universe. What thoughts are racing through your mind right now? Are they thoughts of complaint and scarcity, of disappointment and regret? Or are they thoughts of hope, optimism and faith because you know the Universe listens and wants to give you everything you desire? The Law of Attraction tells us that your thoughts and feelings communicate your desires to the universe, which then mirrors those requests back to you. However, it is important to realize that today's predicament is not tomorrow's future.

Yes, your reality reflects an order that you placed directly with the universe, however unconsciously. No matter how your life looks now, I know you have the power to change it because you can become more conscious, and this is the solution to everything. When you raise your level of consciousness, you come into direct energetic alignment with the energies that shape galaxies and universes and you achieve a wholesome, satisfying and fulfilled life. Just as importantly, you don't have to wait years for these changes to manifest; the secret is that they can happen immediately. In less time than it takes for your heart to thump its beat, you can change your world and your reality.

What change would you like to see first? Is it to create a better balance between work and family? Is it to get out of your comfort zone by expanding your boundaries to unknown and untried territories? Is it to align with your purpose and to positively impact the world? Share your vision at www. thespeedoflightbook.com.

WAKE AND SHAKE UP YOUR DREAMER

Not all those who wander are lost. – J.R.R Tolkien

My grandmother raised me from the time I was 3 months old, and growing up, I often traveled with her to visit her father, who lived in Sylvester, Georgia. We always travelled by bus, and she would take the aisle seat so I could look out the window and dream. Instead of seeing the cotton fields and roadside junk as we drove by, all I saw was the two of us on a giant airplane, flying to fun and exciting places. The roar of the bus became the roar of Niagara Falls, and I saw myself hiking up Mt. Kilimanjaro or even sledding down the Himalayas. If we got talking with other passengers, I always told them I was born and raised in San Francisco because of the Golden Gate Bridge!

After we arrived at my great-grandfather's house and I told him of our adventures, he'd always say 'oh, you are dreamer' and I'd say, 'yes I am!' That simple bus trip was the beginning of my love of travel – throughout my life I've always moved around at a moment's notice, even when I don't know what awaits me in my new home. Great-Grandpa always played along with my long-winded stories of how I'd come to see him this time, so he would always ask how my flight was, and what other adventures I'd had on my way. I'd say we went over the bridge to have lunch with our friends and then climbed the mountains during the 10-minute layover we'd had in Cairo, GA, or some other fanciful tale!

This lifelong love of adventure has driven me to live in places as diverse as New York, Los Angeles and the rainforests of Costa Rica. What are your dreams? What do you want that you do not currently have? Are you secretly envious of those who've quit their jobs in order to travel around the world? Do you wish to write a book? Open a pet store? Be a public speaker?

I call on you to dust off those dreams that lie dormant and unrealized after years of neglect. You are entitled to live the life that only you can dream of; in fact, it's your birthright to live the life of your dreams. Start by speaking about those precious hopes and dreams; giving voice to them is your first step towards making them real. Start by telling me tell me at www.thespeedoflightbook. com. I promise you your dreams will be treated with as much delicate care as the precious jewels they truly are.

TO GET WHAT YOU WANT, MAKE YOUR OWN LUCK

Luck favors the prepared mind. – Louis Pasteur

As you gain clarity and laser-like focus, you will begin to operate in the zone and your life will flow like magic. You will find yourself more and more in the right place at the right time, forging connections with people who have the resources to help you get what you want. It will feel like magic because it will be effortless and it will be easy. The synchronicities will become like beautiful butterflies that show up everywhere, when you learn to thrive in this way.

To be in the flow, you only need to relax and allow. A relaxed mind creates space that allows good things to happen, knowing there is plenty to go around for everyone. You can only put something into a hand that is opened, and thus able to receive, open up to receive what is available to you right now. It is no accident that you are reading this book at this time; I wrote it for you, knowing it would find you when time was right. And the right time for you is now, this very moment. This is the moment when you make the positive and deliberate changes that will impact the rest of your life.

There is abundant evidence of synchronicities that you can see every day. Some chalk it up to luck, but while luck may play a role, a bit of preparation on your part doesn't hurt. It's true that opportunities are always coming your way, but you can only take advantage of them if you are sufficiently prepared. Ask yourself what you need to do to prepare to live your dreams, and then make those things your first priority.

HARNESSING YOUR INTUITIVE MIND

The intuitive mind is a sacred gift, and the rational mind is a faithful servant. We have created a society that honors the servant and has forgotten the gift. - Albert Einstein

We waste so much precious time and energy trying to figure everything out with our rational minds, but the intuitive mind and the mind of God are one and the same. This mind is within all of us, and it has all the answers, if we can just relax and let them emerge. Only God can see the big picture, but we can allow that picture to unfold through our relationship with the God of our own understanding.

Just a glimpse of the big picture is all you need to get the juices flowing. Do not worry about how your vision will unfold, let God be the architect and trust that He will orchestrate outcomes that defy your highest expectations. Keep the faith and keep open - the details will be given as long as you keep your spiritual ear to the ground and follow all the signs you receive.

Intuition is a powerful and miraculous ability to know something and not know why you know it, without any rational proof. You must choose to trust where it leads you, without understanding why.

I like to travel and have fun, so one evening recently I went to the Silver Star Casino in Philadelphia, to try my luck so to speak. On that particular night no one in the gaming section was doing well, and the atmosphere was extremely intense. Personally, I only engage in games of chance when I get that knowing feeling. In that intense atmosphere I just asked myself a simple, silent question: how would I know which slot machine would give me $1000? I don't know where that thought came from or why, but I knew not to ignore this hunch.

I knew that lady luck did not seem to be in the house that night, but my focus didn't waver as I inserted the money and immediately locked the first winning blue, then the second one, and the final jackpot-winning diamond. I had won $1600 with no effort, just by allowing the mind of God to work through me. I couldn't stop laughing and, without reservations, yelled THANK YOU! THANK YOU! I LOVE YOU! I knew I had been rewarded for listening to and trusting the voice of my intuition once again. Eventhough the outer environment was "unfriendly", I relied on my inner compass and it pointed me to the right way.

SOUL HAPPY

Laughter is food for the soul and adds vibrancy to our lives. That's why I always tell my clients to stay light-hearted and not take everything, especially themselves, too seriously. When you learn to find the hidden humor in life, you allow the good vibrations to flow throughout your body. The happier you are, the better you feel, and the deeper your connection will be to your soul.

This link to your soul is so important, because it helps to keeps the rhythm of your life upbeat and promotes a positive attitude, good health, and peak performance. Along with laughing hard and often, think happy and positive thoughts and create a beautiful clutter-free environment for yourself so you can think straight. In the same way that our inner thoughts create our outer reality, the outer space does have an impact on our inner orientation. Which would you naturally prefer? A crowded room filled with unwanted junk or a peaceful zen-like room for meditation? For most of you, I am sure it's the latter because you have room to just breathe and just be.

I cannot overplay the importance of just being. Ever morning, I stay still for a few minutes at the start of each day, to simply contemplate how I will spend your time on this earth in a meaningful way. It's a beautiful practice and while it seems we are doing and achieving nothing, think on this. It's ironic but true that when you take this time, you make more time, because you gain clarity on those priorities that most significantly impact your dreams.

What is the big change your soul deeply and fervently desires to see? If you don't know immediately what it is, give yourself the richness of a few minutes in quiet and solitude and the start of every day. Pretty soon, answers will bubble up from your inner most consciousness. I would love to hear about these whisperings from your soul at www.thespeedoflightbook.com.

THE MEANING OF CHOICE

If you really want to change your life, you must stop doing things that harm you and replace them with expressions of self-love. What do I mean by harmful things? I refer to attitudes like:

- self-deprivation (because you don't deserve more)

- uncalled for sacrifice (because it's expected of you)

- fearing to break out of your limitations (because it's downright scary and who will pick you up when you fall?)

It takes awareness and a conscious decision to shed those harmful habits and attitudes. Understand that it's a step-by-step process, and anyone who really wants to change for the better can do so because there is a wealth of resources available to all of us.

There is a vast amount of information available from the media and internet, and in conversations, books, courses and so forth. With so many resources, how do you choose which to pursue? I prefer the simplest and most effective approach, which is to pursue what resonates with your heart and your intentions for your life. There is nothing greater in life than living from your soul's purpose and passion. I offer a fuss-free, simple method; find out more http://www.thespeedoflightbook.com

With the right tools and intentions, you will be able to enter a higher realm where it will be impossible to return to old ways that no longer serve you. From this place, you will be using your God-given talents, strengths and passions to be totally present in your life, and you will become a beacon to your family, friends, loved ones and the community.

THE DIFFERENCE

In order to live in the flow, we have to clear out mental negativity. Every problem has a solution and the solution always lies in transcending the thinking that caused the problem. If you study people who are living out their dreams, you'll discover that they had to overcome many obstacles, some seemingly surmountable. No human being gets to escape troubles; the key is to realize that you are bigger than any problem and believing in your own strength and potential to find a way around the bumps on the road.

Here are some key characteristics that these heroes tend to share:

- they have skillfully mastered problem-solving in order to get what they want

- they make good decisions;

- they do what's required to get the results they want.

Very often, they establish working relationships with like-minded people and get assistance from others. Successful people know that life is a team sport. They strategically choose to surround themselves with smart people who help them focus on what's right instead of dwelling on what's wrong. Leveraging the energy and resources of a group turbo-charges such smart people towards their goals. You too can travel at warp speed towards your goals. Learn more on how to build the beneficial connections that fast-forward you to your deepest desires and most treasured goals at www.thespeedoflightbook.com.

HARMONY IS SWEET

Harmony is sweet and good for you in every way, just like honey is. Remember that life is one indivisible whole, not just the fragments of your past, present, and future. In recognition of this, be careful to look neither too far back nor too far ahead. When you center your attention on the present moment, you bring all your power to it, and everything works because everything is connected right now.

When the atmosphere is harmonious, it operates free of the negativity that can put a damper on the flow of positive vibrations. Nurture a healthy love of life and honor yourself and the life you have chosen. Fall in love with your life, with where you are now and what you have at this moment. It may not be everything you desire, but when you are in harmony, life becomes much easier. It is very simple - when you are balanced and centered, you attract and manifest that which you desire very quickly.

Stay in a state of admiration and awe of all blessings that are showered on you, be they large or small. Gratitude attracts more of the same, and keeps you in a state of grace. Celebrate your successes, because the attitude of gratitude and appreciation amps up your drive to perform at peak levels to achieve peak results. Everything has its place, and for harmony to exist we must cultivate a pleasant and positive outlook on everything we encounter. Learn more at www.thespeedoflightbook.com

JUST LIKE THE FLOWERS BLOSSOM

Just like flowers, all of us bloom in unique ways at various stages of our lives. You can't compare yourself with anybody else, because they may just be at a different stage than you are. For example, some babies walk at 9 months, 12 months or even 2 years, but they all walk at some point if they are healthy. Honor the uniqueness of who you are, blossoming and coming full-circle like a flower in bloom.

Be mindful and observe yourself as you are thinking, speaking, and acting. If you can begin to catch yourself falling into old patterns and make corrections in the moment, that will go a long way to ensuring that you will bloom into a radiant flower you were meant to be. Oprah Winfrey says, "Breathe. Let go. And remind yourself that this very moment is the only one you know you have for sure."

We are all at different stages of development, and each is equally beautiful in the eyes of God. Learn more at www.thespeedoflightbook.com.

PEOPLE WHO MAKE IT HAPPEN

What will you do with this one and only life you've been given? How can you make your life a blessing to hundreds, or even millions of people? Our legacy is shaped by how we live each day of our lives, and each decision you make. It is one thing to go through the motions of living, and quite another to live a truly extraordinary and meaningful life that fills you with pure joy and soaring exultation.

I encourage you to share that which you have kept sealed and tucked away, and step into your highest ambitions, no matter how impossible they may seem. It is the work of an Authority to help you achieve your dreams, because we see things differently than you do at this moment. Go to www. thespeedoflightbook.com to learn more.

YOUR POSITIVE LEGACY

The fragrance always remains in the hand that gives the rose. – Heda Bejar

Everything you think, do, or say becomes your legacy. There are no guarantees in life, so make sure you are leaving the impression you want to leave on this world each and every day. What meaning will you make of this marvelous life, and what impact will your message have for others?

Maybe you want a life of more leisure, increased income, a new career or you're an entrepreneur seeking more business. If you're a student, maybe you want better grades, or maybe have no idea what you want of life yet. No matter where you are in life, know that nothing is impossible. You have the questions, and the Authority has the answers. Learn more at www.thespeedoflightbook.com.

As an Authority in the field of personal evolution, I can help you to achieve this life by deliberate design. Raise the bar on your personal evolution so you can see results faster than you ever could have imagined or thought possible. Learn to follow your intuition, so you can live your life in the flow and experience a whirlwind of synchronicities that will uplift you into new world beyond your wildest dreams. I invite you to transform in twinkling of an eye, at the speed of light.

Experience is Everything

Create Super Fans and Be Successful Forever

PURDEEP SANGHA

L iving in an increasingly competitive business world has made it harder and harder for startups and small businesses to become and remain successful. No matter the type of product or service, there is always the next great thing or a lower-priced competitor to entice your customers away. Statistics show that only half of new businesses last for at least five years, and a mere third make it to the ten-year mark. And, that's just the companies that get off the ground at all. According to Forbes magazine, about 90% of startups fail. If you're reading this chapter, you are likely a business owner looking to beat those odds. You may even spend a lot of sleepless nights wondering how you can keep your business thriving.

It's important to understand why so many businesses fail. Most often, it is because the owners focus on creating an amazing, cutting-edge product. That is a wonderful idea, that is until someone else comes up with a new cutting-edge feature or finds a way to sell the same product for less. Even if your business is booming, remember that companies fail in an instant, especially those whose owners and management have the mindset that "this will never happen to me or my business."

Instead, business owners need to focus on the one thing that has driven the extraordinary success of Apple, Netflix, and many other of today's most successful corporations: the customer experience. For years, customer experience has been a tool used by many organizations to enhance their business. It's become a discipline similar to marketing and sales. Customer experience is becoming more and more popular now as businesses realize that by delivering a high level of customer experience, they can easily differentiate themselves from their competition. And, when a company creates a product, delivery system or another benefit that enriches the customer's experience, that customer is much more willing to stick with that company for life.

People will pay more to be part of the right experience, even when they can get the same product or service somewhere else for much less. And, those customers are so loyal they wouldn't switch to another competitor even if they were paid to do so. They will also rave about a business on social media or to all their friends and family. Building a base of loyal customers can keep your business successful, and that means significantly less worry for you, the business owner.

Apple has actually created its own culture. Customers line up in front of stores hours in advance of the next iPhone launch to be the first ones with their hands on the product. This kind of devotion comes from more than just wanting a good product – lining up is part of the experience; Apple customers feel they are part of something special. For them, it doesn't get much more exciting than a new iPhone. They will ignore mistakes and faults in a new product so Apple's brand image is never really tarnished. They are Super Fans and they will even advocate for the company among total strangers.

Given how few companies have done a great job of building a substantial base of super-loyal customers, you might think that creating this kind of experience is incredibly difficult – like rocket science. I'm here to tell you that it isn't and that getting Super Fans for your business is easy once you know how. As a Business and Personal Success Coach, I have helped many clients grow to become extremely successful using this strategy. One of my clients currently has people eagerly waiting for his company to create a new product – they don't even care what the product is as long as it comes from his business.

So, how easy is it? Creating Super Fans is not difficult once you stop worrying about your physical product and start thinking about how you want your product to make people feel. It just takes focus, determination, and a little empathy.

CONTROL THE CUSTOMER EXPERIENCE

When you focus on how the consumer feels, you can start to build a strong emotional connection with your customers, and that's what turns them into Super Fans. As a business owner, you will want to control the relationship and the customer experience. To do this, you must lay out the details of how, where, why, when, and what you want your fans to experience. Creating a process for making amazing experiences is crucial, or else your customers could create their own experiences. Since companies are starting to learn the importance of this connection, you will need to develop this advantage over your competitors as quickly as you can.

When many of my clients come to me, they don't know where to start. I tell them to think about creating a connection between themselves and friends. Friends don't just have a single interaction with you. They have a series of interactions that come together to form their journey and connection with you. Acquaintances become friends, and friends become best friends after a series of positive interactions. The process is the same for turning customers into Super Fans. Everyone has a story of their own, and if you, as a business owner, can connect with your customer's story, you can create an emotional bond and convert them into Super Fans.

Here is an example of understanding and controlling your customer's story that comes from my own experience. At one time, I worked in the financial services industry. Our organization offered various products, including mortgages, to our members. Many of our staff viewed the product we were selling at face value, as simply a mortgage, but I explained to them that we were really offering our customers so much more. Our organization was putting our members into homes. We were helping them create an environment in which to raise their families safely. We were offering them a feeling of peace, safety, excitement, and even lifelong memories. In other words, we were providing a wonderful life experience, not just a mortgage. Creating that emotional connection through our marketing and advertising materials is what drove them to do business with our firm instead of any one of the hundreds of other companies on the market that can offer mortgages.

FIND YOUR SUPER FAN'S STORY

Finding the one story that will generate an emotional response from your customers, especially your Super Fans, is important. You can learn a lot by listening to what they have to say. Sometimes, their story may be amazing, and sometimes it may be downright horrible. It is your job to find out what it is and uncover what you can do to make their story even better. For example, if you own a detailing shop or a car dealership and have a fan come in with their Bentley, uncover what the car means to them. It may be a safe vehicle to transport their family, or it may be a source of pride that represents their years of hard work. You will have a completely different conversation with a mother of three children driving a Bentley than you will with a single guy working on Wall Street.

People love talking about themselves, so having these kinds of conversations with fans is not difficult. Ask questions with a genuine interest and people will begin to divulge all kinds of information. Then you are able to cater your offerings based on what you know about your Super Fans and their story.

The key in talking with your Super Fans is to make them feel special. You want to treat all of your customers fairly and equally, but also give them a sense of uniqueness, so treat each of them as your one and only Super Fan. A fan does not care about you or the fact that you own a successful business; they care about themselves. It's human nature to care about yourself first. If you don't believe me, let's do an experiment. Pull up a picture on your phone of you with your family. Before you read any further, please do this. When you just looked at the picture, where did your eyes automatically go? I'm willing to bet that they went to you first. That is what every person does because it's built in us to focus on ourselves. Everyone wants to feel special and unique. You want to satisfy your Super Fans by making them feel like you are always choosing to focus on them first.

The Disney company is an expert at making customers feel special. They have a terminology they use when talking about interacting with their guests. Specifically, employees are either "onstage" or "off stage." When a staff member is interacting with a guest they are considered "onstage," and their role is to cater to that guest on an individual basis. Their single focus is to identify a guest's story and enhance it. There are even signs posted in the staff rooms to remind employees that when they leave the area, they are considered onstage. As a business owner, you need to have the same focus as an employee who is onstage.

THE PSS FORMULA

Making your Super Fans feel special is the driving idea behind the PSS success formula. I created this method after years of research and learning from many organizations, such at MIT and Stanford, and years of studying the best customer service organizations, such as Disney, Zappos, and Toyota. Not-so-good companies dabble in the components of this formula; good companies focus on components of this formula; the best companies integrate this formula into everything that they do; and the industry leader in almost every instance lives, eats and breathes this formula (there is no life for them without it). If you consistently follow this formula, you are guaranteed success.

Here it is:

PSS = People + Strategy + Systems

(Interestingly, my full name is Purdeep Singh Sangha, so my initials match those of the formula!)

Let's start with the strategy because it is what aligns the other two components of the formula with the desired outcome. When many people discuss strategy, they use lots of business jargon to sound intelligent and sophisticated. They want you to think that it is a complicated subject. However, creating Super

Fans is about keeping it simple, so here's the jargon-free explanation: a strategy is simply a map of the journey that you want to take your fans through. (Think of it as one of those treasure maps in the pirate movies you watched as a child.) The strategy outlines the journey from where the customer starts to the final destination, which is where they are converted into Super Fans. Like any good map, it includes some interesting events along the way, as well as some cool characters.

There is no one-size-fits-all method to creating a strategy. Each business has a unique way of getting their fans to the final destination. For example, Tim Hortons creates value by serving customers as fast as they possibly can, while Starbucks encourages their customers to stay in the store for a period of time and enjoy the atmosphere. Both companies have Super Fans, but the strategy for creating and keeping those fans is unique to each company.

The second part of this equation involves focusing on the "people" your Super Fans interact with throughout their experience with your business. Your staff and any third party involved in servicing your Super Fans fall within this category. People can even include animals! Some retail locations have animals because many people, including myself, would sometimes rather pet a dog than interact with the owner, manager or even sales staff. Also, think about mascots at a baseball game – people go crazy over having the opportunity to take a picture with the mascot. For them, interacting with an animal or mascot adds something valuable to the experience.

Systems, the third part of the equation, are the events and vehicles along the journey. The events include every interaction your client has along the way, from the first time they work with your business to the time they find the treasure at the end of the map. Your goal as a business owner is to make these events as easy and painless as possible. For example, in a car dealership, the business owner should make sure buying the car is completed in a single, simple, and pleasant visit. Someone trying to buy a car would not become a return customer if the original process were complex and time-consuming, or if they felt the salesperson was misleading them.

The locations that your customers visit along their journey are also part of the system. These include your offices, retails spaces, website, and social media pages.

THE SUPER STRATEGY

I have created a list of goals that all business owners should have in order to create Super Fans. These goals will help you create what I call the Super Strategy. Let me share with you the first seven of these goals.

Goal #1 is to dream big or go home. The top 1% of athletes, business professionals, and artists are the ones that get the most rewards, so aim to be at the top. If you don't, you will fall short and hit the bottom. If you're reading this, then you have every desire to get to the top. If your business is doing well, great. Dream even bigger and better. If your business is scraping along or just managing to hang on, it can seem difficult to create big goals, but doing it is crucial to turning your business around. See how far you have already come by looking back to before you even started your company. Remember when you had nothing but a dream to be the absolute best in your industry. It was that dream that motivated you to start your business and to get to where you are today. Remembering that dream and building on it will get you through the tough times and back on the track to success.

The only way to amass Super Fans is to absolutely knock the socks off of your customers. Provide a level of customer service that makes them so ecstatic they can't wait to do more business with you, and to tell everyone they know about their experience. Whether you are one person running your business, or you have a team of thousands, you can do this – believe in yourself! Put customers first, and you'll do big things.

Goal #2 is to remember the end goal! Just like anything else in life, if you don't know where you're going, it's going to be tough to get there. I've asked many executives the question, "What's your end goal?" throughout the years and their answers often make me laugh. They say things that are so convoluted that it's difficult to make any sense of what their goal actually is! Keep your goals simple so that everybody in your organization can understand them. The end goal of any business should be to create Super Fans. Having Super Fans means that you can wake up every morning seeing your customers rave about your product and services, knowing that they are completely loyal to your business. When you have Super Fans, you don't have to worry about how to replace lost customers (because you won't really have any) and you can focus on creating amazing experiences for others, which will bring you a huge amount of joy.

Goal #3 is to be genuine. In order to successfully get Super Fans, you must genuinely care about your customers and make them successful at what they want to accomplish (e.g., get sales, speak professionally or take beautiful pictures that capture their travel adventures), as well as connect with them emotionally. Focus on providing the best level of customer service and success will follow. If you are 100% genuine, people will see your vision and feel what you are trying to achieve. Then, they will be behind you and support you every step of the way.

Goal #4 is that you must invest in creating Super Fans. I have worked with clients whose main focus is to cut costs while making as many sales as possible. But, long-term success is not all about the sales. Making your customers happy will cost some money but, the more you invest in creating Super Fans, the more you will get back in return. Just like any relationship, you must first give before you receive.

Goal #5 is that experience trumps all! Many larger organizations argue that sales and marketing are more important to the success of an organization than maximizing the customer experience. They believe that spending more on branding or salesforce efforts will generate more sales than customer relationship building. I call that BS! How many times have you, as a consumer, been sold an item based on its marketing and then been disappointed by the product? How did this make you feel? Marketing can often set unrealistic expectations for a product, and leave a customer feeling disappointed. Disappointed customers do not feel compelled to become return customers or to refer their closest friends and family members.

Future Shop and Best Buy are prime examples of how sales strategies can hinder or help the customer experience. Both stores are known as big places to buy electronics. Future Shop pays its employees commission, so when you walk through the door, you are bombarded by aggressive salespeople. This causes customers to avoid shopping there again. Best Buy, on the other hand, pays its employees an hourly wage so they can focus on providing customers an enjoyable experience instead of trying to make a quick sale. My guess is that many of you have never even heard of Future Shop because so many of them are closing. Best Buy is still around.

Goal #6 is to focus on the 20%. There's a popular business principle that 80% of the efforts, time, or resources spent in a business lead to 20% of results. Vice versa, 20% of the efforts, time and resources lead to 80% of the outcomes. That's because businesses most often concentrate on the whole potential marketplace, rather than the frequent or repeat purchasers of their products. This principle holds true for getting Super Fans. Whatever your desired outcome is, whether it's profits, growth, market share, etc. you need to focus on the 20% of your customers that help you accomplish your goal. Trying to get 100% of your customers to the Super Fan level would be frustrating and impossible, and it would cause you to waste a lot of resources. Instead, focus on your best customers – the 20% that account for the 80% of the results you are looking for. Imagine what shifting 80% of unproductive resources to productive ones could do for your business. It would be a massive transformation. Corporations are hesitant to do this because of the enormous impact it would have on the people within the organization. High-paying positions might go away because large corporate hierarchies are often inefficient. Small businesses are much more likely to make these kinds of transformative moves.

A simple example of the 80/20 principle involves the gym. The three main exercises that give you 80% of the results are bench presses, squats, and deadlifts. Most people spend about 20% of their time doing these exercises and the other 80% of their time doing exercises that are not that productive. I used to do the same thing when I was younger, even though I was a certified trainer. I spent a lot of time doing fancy exercises that I thought would get results but just weren't. When I shifted my focus to spending 50% of my time doing the three key exercises, I experienced dramatic outcomes. My workouts became simpler, I had a stronger focus, and I was able to measure my outcomes much easier. I reduced the complexity by 50% and increased my productivity by at least 50%.

You must be willing to give the 20% that represents your Super Fans' extra attention, to do things out of the norm, and maybe even bend the rules a little. For this 20%, you should be willing to do almost anything because they generate 80% of your results. They are the ones keeping your company profitable and letting you have peace of mind about your business. Remember that these are also the customers you can charge a premium for the amazing experiences you provide them.

The 20% is also the group that will give the best referrals and attract even more fans. The people being referred often have a profile similar to that of your Super Fans. As the old saying goes, "birds of a feather flock together." Those who were referred are probably already familiar with your products, the value, and the cost. Most of your selling has already been done by your Super Fans. What more could you ask for?!

For a small business owner, determining who the 20% are should not be too complicated. It should take a day or two to analyze sales, profits, and expenses to determine your Super Fans. If profit is your focus, your 20% most profit-driving customers would be your Super Fans. If stability is your focus, then determine who the most loyal fans are – those who have been with you the longest or repurchase more often.

Goal #7 is to give everyone a great experience. Focusing on the 20% is important to achieve 80% of the results, but keep in mind that even one person trashing your business can have a severe negative impact on your success. Thus, it is important that everyone has an awesome experience. Maybe you won't bend the rules as much or give them the little bit of extra attention, but you still need to make sure that every interaction with your business is pleasurable. So many organizations treat their top percentile as kings and queens and everyone else like peasants. Although common, this is a bad business practice that has consequences.

It is also important to remember that your normal fans can become Super Fans! As long as you treat them right and create an emotional attachment, they could easily become part of your top 20%!

IT'S EASIER THAN YOU THINK!

I know I said this before, but it is important and so bears repeating. Let me remind you of the first goal I mentioned, which was to dream big. Mark Zuckerberg and Elon Musk probably had no idea how successful their companies would become, but they did have a dream that drove them. Whatever your business goals are, I know that you can achieve them.

There is so much opportunity to create Super Fans and so many companies that still focus on sales instead of an experience. That leaves the door open for you to get ahead of your competition, especially if you act fast.

You don't have to spend hundreds of thousands of dollars to create a great experience for your customers. You also don't have to be a marketing genius or a fabulous salesperson. If you create an awesome experience for your fans, they will do all of the selling and marketing for you. Dedication, focus, politeness, and empathy go a long way in business.

There are many more goals and recommendations in the Super Strategy, and they are outlined in my book *Super Fans: How To Create Unwavering Customer Loyalty*. I also coach business owners, executives and managers. For more detailed information, please feel free to check out my book and subscribe to my newsletters at www.CreateSuperFans.com.

Motivation Does Activate and Sustain Behaviour

How to Bring Results in Life and Business

JULIE HOGBIN

B efore we talk about motivation in any great detail, it would be a good idea to cover the basics about what motivation really is. There are many, many, theories and huge amounts of research has been conducted on the subject over many decades. To be honest, with all the information out there it can be confusing as to what it all means.

One thing is for sure, one theory — one piece of information — does not cover it all as each researcher has their own bent and interpretation on the subject. It is when you are able to link it all together that it starts to make sense and you are able to do something with the information to help yourself.

I have researched, read about, practiced, and taught this subject to over 20,000 Leaders in Life, Business and the Entrepreneur market, both one-on-one and in small groups for very nearly three decades, and I am still learning.

This chapter is based around my knowledge, my interpretation, and a definition of Motivation that I have worked with for a long time. I have neither found nor developed a better definition — yet!

"Motivation is a conscious or unconscious driving force that arouses and directs action towards the achievement of a desired goal."

ClaimYourDestiny.global   #ConsciousLeadership

So, what does this mean in reality? It means that we are motivated by internal and external factors and that sometimes we know what those factors are and sometimes we don't: Our actions and thoughts are both conscious and unconscious in nature. It also means that the motives provoke a reaction and an action that help us 'get' something we want — a goal — and as a driving force they are powerful.

So my 1st questions to you are:

- What is your goal?

- What are you working towards?

- How many goals do you have?

- What is driving you?

- How conscious are you?

Motivation is an internal force; we are the only ones who can motivate us. Motivation can be affected by external influences. Ultimately it is us, and only us, that make the decision to do or not to do something. Nobody can make you feel or do anything! It is your absolute choice to capitulate and do, or to resist and not do.

We make the decision based on the information we have at the time and how confident we feel. There are many emotions and personal characteristics that come into play when we are talking about motivation and all that entails.

When we say that others motivate us what it really means is that they have created an environment that inspires us to do something. We make the decision out of fear in some cases, because we know it makes sense in other cases, because we aspire to be like the individual, or, more simply, just because we want to.

For you, and everybody else, your desired goal always provides you with a positive outcome. It gives you something you want even if that want is unconsciously driven. For others viewing it from their perspective, that outcome may be viewed as negative.

Let me explain what I mean with a couple of examples.

Addicts of any description do whatever it takes to fuel their need. They are achieving their desired outcome with more alcohol, more food, less food, more drugs, or just more of something, and they will go to extreme lengths to get it, such as selling personal and other people's belongings, lying and deceiving, going into debt and stealing.

Someone comes home with great intent of doing some research, maybe to write a book or to do some personal development such as going to the gym, and they end up sitting in front of the TV for hours with a bottle of wine. What is their driving force? We may not understand it as the viewer but there is definitely one for the person being observed.

Let's look at a couple of positive examples with a more generally accepted encouraging outcome.

A young person decides what they want to achieve in their life. They study like crazy to get the grades required to get to the top university and to study in a class of four with the top professor in their subject matter field, and they achieve it.

An individual from an underprivileged background wants to change their life, achieve greater things than have ever been achieved in their family, and become independently wealthy, and they are successful in achieving their goals.

Now for every example shared the opposite can be true as well. Not everybody becomes an addict, not everyone slouches in front of the TV, not every student achieves their potential, and not every underprivileged individual becomes independently wealthy.

"Everything you do is goal-driven. Everything you do is because you want the end result — whatever that end result may be!"

ClaimYourDestiny.global   #ConsciousLeadership

The examples are all based on how motivated the individual is to achieve their goal. Now if you know your goal consciously, can keep it in focus and resist the temptation of your old ways, you can achieve marvellous results.

The rest of this chapter will look at what drives you and how you can change your habits and behaviours over a period both short and long term, with the aim to achieve whatever it is you want.

I reference no theory in this chapter. There are many to read and learn which are of use to us all intellectually and unless the theory is practically applied and interpreted into reality all they remain are theories. I have spent decades interpreting theories into real life behaviours that make a difference for the better.

A few more questions for you to think about first.

- What are your drivers?

- What are your values?

- What is your risk tolerance?

- How much do you want to fit in with the 'norm' of your social group?

- How much do you really want, on a scale of 1 to 10, the thing it is you are aiming to achieve?

- How comfortable are you with change?

There are a lot more questions to ask but these will start you on the journey to understand your own motivators.

"Your motives create your habits, for good and bad, as they are your driving force."

ClaimYourDestiny.global   #ConsciousLeadership

There is so much information coming at us on a minute by minute basis. We make thousands upon thousands of decisions every day — so many in fact, we cannot be conscious of all the decisions, to do or not to do something, that we do make. We would be completely overwhelmed if we did.

So what do we do? We create patterns of behaviour that we do not have to think about, as it is quicker that way, to achieve our outcomes. We create habits that get us what we want in the easiest manner.

"Your habits have created your behaviour through your values, beliefs, and attitudes."

ClaimYourDestiny.global   #ConsciousLeadership

HABITS

Habits are a set of thoughts, behaviours, and ways of being that are developed through repeated behaviour. Habits are formed from the moment we become aware that there is a 'norm' of how to do things. Some we pick up from our parents, guardians, siblings, and influential individuals around us at a very early age. Others we develop for ourselves through the maturing process.

"Look to your parents for your beliefs about the world and yourself – you may be amazed at the similarities."

ClaimYourDestiny.global   #ConsciousLeadership

Once habits are created they can be difficult to break. To break a habit, we must consciously think about doing something different and then do it — which can equal hard work and being uncomfortable.

The thing is, we can all break habits if we really want to. BUT (and there is a big BUT) the unconscious part of our being is there to keep us safe. Any change and it may feel we are under threat and revert quickly to the old ways.

"Talk to your unconscious and ask its permission if you want to change some deep held habits and motivations to do things in a new way."

"Sounds a bit weird? Well it works, try it for yourself."

ClaimYourDestiny.global   #ConsciousLeadership

VALUES

Your values are a central part of who you are and who you want to be. By becoming more aware of these driving motivators in your life, you can use them as a guide to make the best choice in any situation.

Your decisions and actions, when in line with your values, will be easy to make and put into practice. If you are attempting to do something that is not held as a value to you, you will find it harder to do and, potentially, you will be in conflict with yourself.

Here is an example. If one of your values is honesty and you are in a relationship, business or personal, with someone who you know tells untruths, how hard will you find it to trust them? What will this do to your behaviour and your motivation within the relationship?

Values can be worked with, reordered, and installed — so do not lose hope. I personally have needed to work hard on my value regarding money. To say the least, it was slightly askew!

ATTITUDES

Your attitude is a predisposition to respond either negatively or positively towards an idea, object, person, or situation. It is the way you feel about something or someone. It can also be a particular feeling or opinion. It is seen as a conscious behaviour but will come from an unconscious driver.

Your attitude evolves as a result of your beliefs and values and will influence:

- Your choice of action and behaviour

- Your response to challenges

- Your response to incentives

- Your response to a word

- Your response to someone trying to help you

We all have an attitude — we cannot not have one. Generally, when it is said someone has an attitude it is meant as a negative opinion, but attitudes are drivers for good as well. It is just a common adaptation of a word which is more often linked to negativity.

As with anything else we do, our attitude is a choice we make. My choice, and I trust yours as you are reading this book, is to start each day with a positive attitude — it soon becomes a habit.

If you want to change something in your life, surround yourself with those who are on the same path or learn from those who have already done the 'thing' that you want to do. Attitudes are contagious so eradicate those personally held by yourself and those that are owned by people that may be in your circle who aren't helping you. If you don't know what your attitudes are, ask someone for feedback who will tell you the truth.

Also carefully study your close associates to make your own decisions on who stays with you on your journey and who leaves, their attitudes can be contagious. Look at the relationships that are in your life and acknowledge whether they are supporting you or hindering you. Decisions then can be made from a realistic position of what you want to do.

SOCIAL INTELLIGENCE

Social intelligence indicates that portions of our knowledge acquisition can be directly related to observing others within the context of social interactions, experiences and media influences.

So what does this mean to all of us? Basically, it means that if we see something that is rewarded, we copy it so that we get rewarded. We achieve the same result as we have observed, therefore we have achieved our result, which was our goal. There is far more to it but that's the basic concept. We learn by example from others.

So who do we copy? We copy those close to us and we adopt behaviours to fit into the crowd and belong. As we get older, we copy those who we admire or those who we aspire to be like. We develop a sense of self and become more aware of what it is we want. We begin to lead rather than follow — well some of us do and I expect you are a leader since you are reading this book! Join my Facebook group for more, https://www.facebook.com/groups/ClaimYourDestiny/

We are motivated to belong to a group with a certain set of characteristics.

That could be because it is what we want or it can be because we know no different. It can be through peer pressure or choice, but whichever route we take it is ultimately our choice!

Join my Facebook group for more, https://www.facebook.com/groups/ClaimYourDestiny/

It is these drivers of behaviour that make you act differently from, or the same as, others in any given situation. So, by understanding these drivers, you can better understand why you do the things you do. The skill is not only to understand your conscious needs, but also those that are unconscious in nature.

"In the choice between changing one's mind and proving there's no need to do so, most people get busy on the proof."

-John Kenneth Galbraith

SELF-PERCEPTION

Self-perception is the belief or disbelief in our own capabilities to achieve a goal or an outcome. These beliefs provide the foundation for human motivation, well-being, and personal accomplishment. This is because unless you believe that your actions can produce the outcomes you desire, you will have little incentive to act or to persevere in the face of difficulties.

Of course, human functioning is influenced by many factors. The success or failure you experience as you engage the countless tasks that comprise your life naturally influences the many decisions you must make. Also, the knowledge and skills you possess will certainly play critical roles in what you choose to do and not do.

"People's level of motivation, emotional states, and actions are based more on what they believe than on what is objectively true. For this reason, how you behave can often be better predicted by the beliefs you hold about your capabilities than by what you are actually capable of accomplishing."

ClaimYourDestiny.global   #ConsciousLeadership

You only need to watch one of the reality TV shows to see how clearly some people are deluded about their own abilities. The opposite is also true — you talk to someone who you know is gifted and they think and believe the complete opposite.

Our upbringing and early influencers, or even a recent happening, have a huge part to play in how and what we believe about ourselves. The great news though is whatever has happened in the past does not have to happen in our future.

These perceptions help determine what you do with the knowledge and skills you have. They also explain why your behaviours are sometimes not matched to your actual capabilities and why your behaviour may differ widely from somebody else, even when you have similar knowledge and skills.

For example, many talented people suffer frequent (and sometimes debilitating) bouts of self-doubt about capabilities they clearly possess, just as many individuals are confident about what they can accomplish despite possessing a modest repertoire of skills. Belief and reality are seldom perfectly matched, and individuals are typically guided by their beliefs when they engage the world.

As a consequence, your accomplishments are generally better predicted by your self-perception than by your previous achievements, knowledge, or skills. Of course, no amount of confidence or self-appreciation can produce success when requisite skills and knowledge are absent.

"Skills and knowledge can all be gained if you want them enough and you find the right mentor to teach you."

ClaimYourDestiny.global   #ConsciousLeadership

COLLECTIVE PERCEPTION

Because individuals operate collectively as well as individually, self-perception is both a personal and a social construct. Collective systems develop a sense of collective effectiveness, it can create the group's shared belief in its capability to attain goals and accomplish desired tasks.

One brain is one but the collective brainpower of a group equals more than the sum of its parts — it's the adage $1+1=3$ or $2+2 = 5$. However, this is only true when the collective works together in harmony with the same aim. If members of the collective are working against each other one brain doesn't even equate to one — it will function at a lesser capability, as will the individual as they will be experiencing conflict.

For example, organisations develop collective beliefs about the capability of their salesforce to perform, of their managers to teach and otherwise enhance the lives of their workforce, and of their administrators and policymakers to create environments conducive to these tasks. Organisations, as well as individuals, also create beliefs that are not positive — they cannot gain additional sales, clients, revenue, etc. Collectiveness creates a culture which needs to be managed.

Organisations with a strong sense of positive collective perception exercise empowering and vitalising influences over their employees. These effects are evident in their results.

The power of others' attitudes (as mentioned previously) are contagious and will affect your motivation. If you are in the company of a high sender of negative emotion, you will be affected. If you are in the company of a high sender of positivity, it will be less influential.

As the saying goes, it only takes one bad apple to spoil the barrel.

Weed out the bad apples and your motivation will improve. Take on more of the good apples that are doing the same thing that you want to do and your motivation will improve by leaps and bounds.

CHOICES

Only you can justify the choices you make and most of you will make your choices in reference to past experiences rather than future opportunities. Change how you think and you will change your future.

"The definition of insanity is doing the same thing over and over again and expecting a different result."

– Albert Einstein

How do you change to get a different result? It's easy, think differently and take different actions. Open your mind and your being to possibilities; your past does not have to equal your future. With #ConsciousLeadership it can all change.

Every thought, every action, and every decision you make takes you closer to, or further away, from where you want to be. The smallest of decisions compounded over time creates massive change. Rather than attempt to make a huge change overnight, which can be scary and overwhelming, make small incremental changes that lead you towards your goal.

What do I mean? 5 minutes exercise a day wont make much difference if you do or don't do it BUT 5 minutes everyday will. A cake on one day wont make much difference to your health BUT a cake every day will (in the wrong direction). Delaying cutting the lawn for one day wont make much difference BUT delaying every day will.

Even doing nothing takes you further away because everything else is moving forward. The skills of yesteryear will not suffice in the next year. Think about how technology changes. If you haven't kept up with the last change you will soon be a very long way behind!

Sometimes, it can be a life-changing event that allows you to make the decision to do something immediately that you have tried before and failed at. A friend of mine, when diagnosed with cancer, stopped smoking overnight after 40 years. Please do not leave it until that type of thing happens before you change. Take on board #ConsciousLeadership now and change your life for the better, it is your choice!

Start to work now on different decisions for what you want and need:

- Why wait to be taken through a disciplinary process at work before you improve your skills or performance?

- Why wait until you are so over or underweight before you change your nutrition intake?

- Why wait until you cannot walk upstairs without puffing before you increase your fitness level?

- Why wait until you are close to retirement to think about how much money you need to live on and enjoy your retirement?

Through reading, applying, and practicing the experiences of others, you can learn what has worked for those before you, and you can apply those principles in your own life.

Motivational states are directive, they guide behaviours toward satisfying specific goals or specific needs. Do you have clearly defined goals? If you don't, sit down now, identify what it is you really want or need, and write that down. Then create a plan of how you will achieve it. This will provide you with motivation to do things differently.

If you want more information on how to this, I can highly recommend my book 'The Life Changing Magic of Setting Goals'. It is available from Amazon or through ClaimYourDestiny.global

"Change begins with your awareness that your beliefs are a choice; all beliefs, conscious or unconscious, are based on a choice."

ClaimYourDestiny.global   #ConsciousLeadership

There are a myriad of choices to be made all of the time. If you choose a different way to do something, gather information that allows you to make an educated choice for action. Do your research and due diligence and pick the best solution for you.

This will enhance your confidence, create new knowledge, quieten the inner doubting voice, match your values, enhance your beliefs, or question them to bolster your attitude.

This will allow you to convince your unconscious that you are looking after it and it will help you. Provide your unconscious with the reason why you are making alternate choices to that of the past and it will support you all the way.

DELAYED GRATIFICATION

There have been many studies done related to the benefits of delayed gratification. What does this really mean? It means living with the future in mind rather than the present.

In this world of instant gratification, keeping up with the Joneses, wearing the right designer labels, being influenced by adverts that say you must have this face cream and that aftershave, feeling like your holidays must become bigger and more expensive, having to change your car every two years, etc. It can be hard to resist the instant temptation, to be outside the norm, or to exclude yourself from your friends' activities.

In the moment, sometimes it can seem obvious to take the reward, and worry about the future in the future.

Your choice is dependent on your goals, your drivers, your beliefs (and how strong they are), and how strong your will to resist temptation is.

If you can recognise when you have an opportunity for a larger or more important reward, it shows you know the difference between your needs and your wants. When you can recognise these situations, there are key terms you must think of.

Patience, will, and self-control are all characteristics of people who are masters of their environment. One common challenge is postponing immediate gratification in the pursuit of long-term goals. Delayed gratification is the process of transcending immediate temptations to achieve long-term goals.

Knowing how to create, manage, and control your goals is the first step towards completing the things you want most in life; with a goal, we engage our brain to work toward it.

Think of goals as roadmaps designed to keep you on target. They make the experience and the journey possible and more enjoyable. They, in fact, become priorities that drive our actions. They become motivators.

Let me ask you once again:

- What are your long-term goals? And for some of you

- What are your short-term goals?

If you do not have goals sit down now and plan them for yourself, tell yourself and others they are important, write them down and believe you are worthy of them and you will achieve them. Focus on them and they will become a reality

THE POWER OF QUESTIONS

Questions, when constructed in the right way, are the most powerful way to access your beliefs. And this works irrespective of who asks the question. Ask yourself a question and your mind will do its best to provide you with an answer. The better your question, the better the answer.

Do you want to spend the rest of your life figuring out how to get the things you desire, or would you rather put all the guesswork behind you and get down to the fun of building an out-of-this-world lifestyle? Easy choice, right? Then do yourself a favour: suspend your disbelief, lower your shields, and try a simple way of improving your life.

Identify someone you respect who's already experiencing what you're after, find out what questions they habitually ask themselves to achieve those experiences, then use those questions yourself.

This is a globally powerful approach to success that can get you the things you want more quickly than anything else I've discovered. The habitual questions that others ask themselves when asked by yourself, to yourself can transform your life. You don't even need to understand how it all works really, although the answer's quite simple:

"When you change your habitual questions, you change your beliefs, when you change your beliefs, you change your actions, when you change your actions you change your results."

ClaimYourDestiny.global   #ConsciousLeadership

Try it! Take the time to prove to yourself that it works, that it can change the level of pain and pleasure in your life. If you like the results, keep using the questions you've discovered until they become second nature. Do this and you won't care about the why's and the wherefore's. You'll be too busy! You'll have learned firsthand there's nothing more powerful than a good question followed by action.

Ask different questions, and you will end up thinking different thoughts, saying different words, taking different actions, and getting different results. When you go one step further by modeling the questions of successful people, you're helping to ensure that the different results you're pursuing are also good results. In other words, you've done everything you can to arrive at a different place — a good place — to develop different beliefs, which are also profitable beliefs, and to become a different person who is more like the people you admire.

FOCUS

So what does all this mean really?

It means that by looking at why you do what you do and the beliefs behind that, you can basically change the thoughts and motives that direct your behaviour so that you achieve a different result, start a new job, get a promotion, create your own business, leave a relationship, start a relationship, have that difficult conversation, learn to swim, fly a plane, or simply eat a new food; the list is endless.

It is your choice completely — where your focus goes your energy flows — so change your focus to change your results.

Some of our important choices have a timeline. If you delay a decision, the opportunity is gone forever. Sometimes your doubts will stop you from making a choice that involves change and an opportunity may be missed. If you really truly want to change, start now — now is as good a time as any.

Create and ClaimYourDestiny.global through #ConsciousLeadership

My Facebook page and group is ClaimYourDestiny or you can follow me on Twitter @JulieHogbin. Visit ClaimYourDestiny.global for more articles and up to date information, plus various other social media channels and Linkedin. My hashtag is #ConsciousLeadership if you would like to find me.

Motives and motivation are a matter of choice — yours! Choose well, look at why you believe what you believe, and question it. Listen to the answers of the questions you ask and you will create a different future if you really want to.

My final questions to you are:

- How much do you want to change?

- How willing are you to do what is required?

- What do you need to do right now?

Good luck with whatever it is you want to do. Here's to your fabulous success; you know where to find me.

Julie xx

.

www.ingramcontent.com/pod-product-compliance
Lightning Source LLC
Chambersburg PA
CBHW031328210326
41519CB00048B/3596

TAKE CHARGE FOR A POSITIVE LIFE

Shifting your thinking requires action. Learn how to achieve all you desire in *Five Key Elements for Success,* a proven strategy to achieve your desire over and over — with ease and happiness.

Alana Leone shares the tools needed to help you do just that. Right from the start, she acknowledges that we all carry negative baggage from our past experiences. Her goal is to help you learn the skills necessary to clear out the negative emotions associated with those experiences.

Alana's *Five Key Elements for Success* include more than just clearing the negative. The book also focuses on how to bring the positive into your life by taking control of your thoughts and making choices that shift your responses to various events in your life. Change happens with taking action, now!

Along the way, Alana also introduces you to her 'Pushy Coaching & Training' experience, which allows you to enjoy the benefits of her coaching. No matter who you are or where you are in your life, Alana can help you get to the next level!

ABOUT THE AUTHOR

Alana is a world authority in shifting thinking. She believes that by clearing past emotions you can free your mind from negative noise and live in ease and happiness now. She wants to help you get laser focused on your desires and take action to accomplish them.

She has trained with the best in the world in her field, from names like Dr. Richard Bandler, Blair Singer, Marcia Wieder, Drs. Tad, and Adriana James, to name a few. She also works with the world's leading seminar company, Success Resources America. With her passion she inspires people to pursue their every desire and live with a shift in success.

She is an author, trainer, entrepreneur, and owner of 'Pushy Coaching & Training.'

ISBN 978-1-77277-249-4

USD $19.95 CDN $24.95 UK £14.95